Henry Kissinger

Biography

The Life, Power, and Politics of a Global Diplomat

Chris D Garcia

TABLE CONTENTS

Chapter 1: The Making of Henry Kissinger

FÜRTH ON BOTH SIDES OF THE ATLANTIC

On May 27, 1923, Henry Kissinger was born in the Bavarian town of Fürth. Heinz Alfred was the first child of Louis Kissinger, a schoolteacher, and Paula Stern, the daughter of Falk Stern, a wealthy cattle merchant who helped the Kissingers buy their first home. The Kissingers were devout Orthodox Jews, staunch Republicans, and solidly middle-class German patriots. Kissinger grew up in what appeared to be a safe and secure community with his younger brother, Walter, developing a lifelong passion for soccer, reading voraciously, and enduring the other learning rituals of German Bildung, or "inward cultivation," including piano lessons, which the young Heinz despised. His parents had close friends from Fürth's small Jewish community, which could trace its beginnings back to the fifteenth century and whose emancipation and active participation in town life stretched back more than seventy-five years.

As secure as this world appeared to be, it was on the verge of collapsing. The earliest warning flags appeared in the year Kissinger was born. Germans used wheelbarrows full of cash to buy bread when their currency collapsed under the weight of World War I reparations and the French occupation of the Ruhr. Adolf Hitler attempted his "Beer Hall Putsch" in Munich, only a few hundred miles from Fürth, in November, failing to topple the Weimar Republic but displaying the intensity of nationalist opposition and the possibility for anti-Semitic violence. Heinz Kissinger had no recollection of the hardships of Weimar democracy. His family's financial situation was unaffected by inflation or the start of the Great Depression in 1929. The rise of the Nazis to power in January 1933, on the other hand, made its mark. His father lost his teaching job and became immobile and psychologically depressed.

3

"Permanently retired," Louis Kissinger "withdrew into his study," according to his son Walter. As a young teenager, Kissinger and his brother witnessed the progressive segregation, isolation, and humiliation that the Jews of Fürth faced; even attending soccer games risked being pummelling by young Nazi thugs. The environment of Heinz's youth quickly crumbled, and his parents and the elder generation of Fürth's Jews were unable to shield their children from the hostility that surrounded them. Kissinger's mother began looking for a way out of Germany when the Nuremberg Laws were passed in 1935. A cousin in the United States was willing to provide the financial help the Kissingers needed to emigrate. After a final visit with Paula's elderly parents in Leutershausen, where Heinz witnessed his father cry for the first time, the family left for New York in August 1938. Only three months later, on Kristallnacht, the synagogue in Fürth, along with hundreds of others across Germany, was burned to the ground in a night of planned brutality. Fewer than forty Jews remained in Fürth in 1945, out of a population of over two thousand in 1933. The Holocaust would claim at least thirteen, if not more, members of Kissinger's family.

Kissinger romanticised his early experiences in America after achieving prominence. He frequently recalled the story of strolling down the street, seeing a gang of youngsters, and then crossing the street to avoid the anticipated violence, only to realise he was in America. As appealing as this fiction is, the reality of New York in the late 1930s was far from peaceful. Ethnic conflict was not uncommon. America in the late 1930s was more of a hostile and apathetic environment, absorbed with its own pain and seeking to isolate itself from the rest of the world. Despite the fact that Franklin D. Roosevelt's New Deal was in its sixth year, unemployment remained over 20%, and immigrants were neither plentiful nor desired by the majority of Americans. Although the Kissingers were lucky to have family in New York, their living conditions were challenging. They lived in a modest two-bedroom apartment in the

Bronx for the first two years. In 1940, they relocated to a larger apartment at 615 Fort Washington Avenue in Washington Heights, a neighbourhood in Manhattan known as the "Fourth Reich" because it attracted so many Germans. Louis Kissinger developed gallbladder problems and fell deeper into depression, telling his wife that he was the "loneliest person in this big city." Despite the fact that he eventually got work as a bookkeeper, Paula was in charge. Paula became a caterer with the support of the Council of Jewish Women and quickly created a small business that helped keep the family financially stable.

Kissinger struggled to establish friends in America. He began dating Anneliese Fleischer, a fellow Nuremberg refugee, albeit their relationship developed slowly and patchily. Kissinger attended night classes at City College of New York after graduating from George Washington High School. During the day, he worked in a brush-cleaning plant owned by his mother's family, and he looked headed for a future as an accountant, "a nice job," he later said. In the words of one biographer, "Nothing that happened to Kissinger during those years encouraged him to read more widely; his historical interests were as underdeveloped when he was twenty as when he arrived in New York as a boy of fifteen."

THE UNITED STATES ARMY AND MR. HENRY

In January 1943, Henry Kissinger received his draft notice and became a part of an unparalleled time in American history—the mobilisation of around 16 million Americans, or more than 10% of the population, for the first genuinely global combat. This mobilisation resulted in unimaginable agony, with about 400,000 Americans killed and countless more injured, both physically and psychologically. Nonetheless, it would be a hugely liberating experience for millions of Americans, including both of the Kissinger brothers, who, despite travelling much, had never left their insular society. The geographical and social mobility unleashed by

World War II, aided by the GI Bill's financial and educational benefits, dramatically transformed the United States, not only establishing it as the first superpower but also opening up unparalleled opportunities for millions of its residents.

Without World War II, Kissinger's career would be impossible to envision. Kissinger was assigned to the Infantry Replacement Training Center in Spartanburg, South Carolina, following his induction. In the words of one writer, "The army experience, which for so many Americans meant death or a hiatus in their prospective careers, meant a new life for Henry Kissinger." This weird new environment enthralled and horrified him, and he shared with his brother the resentments of an unhappy draftee who had been "pushed around and inoculated, counted, and stood at attention." Despite subsequently expressing his admiration for "the middle Americans" from "Wisconsin, Illinois, and Indiana" with whom he trained, he warned Walter, "Don't become too friendly with the scum you invariably meet there." Continuing his warnings, he advised his younger brother to avoid gambling and prostitutes, particularly the "filthy, syphilis-infected camp followers." He also advised Walter to "repress your natural tendencies and don't push them to the forefront." Kissinger, on the other hand, stood out in a different way. Kissinger performed well enough in a set of Army tests administered at Clemson University to be assigned to the Army Specialized Training Program (ASTP), which sent talented troops to colleges. Along with this legal recognition of his brilliance, Henry Kissinger became an American citizen on June 19, 1943.

Kissinger was sent by the ASTP program to study engineering at Lafayette College in Easton, Pennsylvania, which was only approximately eighty miles west of his Washington Heights home. Kissinger finished twelve engineering courses in a little more than six months, which was anticipated of ASTP students. Despite his heavy labour, he hitchhiked home on occasion, saw his girlfriend, and religiously attended synagogue with his father.

Kissinger's ASTP experience validated his growing confidence in his own intellectual talents, but it may also have been the start of his religious misgivings. By "eating ham for Uncle Sam," Kissinger defied his Orthodox community's definition of his identity and completed his "Americanization," discarding his religion but retaining his German accent, his acute mind distinguishing him inside the melting pot. Kissinger rose to academic prominence as a visibly brilliant student on whom teachers relied to clarify complicated things to the other soldiers. When the Army cancelled the ASTP program and returned the trainees to their humble rank as privates due to the manpower needs of D-Day in Europe, Kissinger was among the twenty-five men chosen to be examined for entrance to medical school. He was not picked as one of the final five, due to a quota system that allowed just one Jewish student among the two Protestants and two Catholics. Kissinger was deployed to Camp Claiborne, Louisiana, and the Eighty-fourth Infantry Division, along with 2,800 ASTP trainees, on April 1, 1944. The drill sergeants handled the "college kids" unmercifully on April Fools' Day, adding to the ASTP soldiers' sense of victimhood. Kissinger became lonely during arduous training sessions in the Louisiana heat, calling collect to say, "Mother, I want to walk out on my hands and crawl home."

Even in the desolation of Camp Claiborne, Kissinger stood out, having been chosen by his commanders to offer soldiers a weekly briefing on war news. Kissinger was more struck with Fritz Kraemer, an elderly German refugee in an American uniform, who came to Camp Claiborne in May 1944 to speak on the purpose of the war. Kissinger wrote Kraemer a message after his passionate speech: "Dear Private Kraemer: I heard you talk the day before. This is the proper procedure. "Can I assist you in any way?" Kraemer reacted almost instantly to the simple "fan letter," returning a few days later to seek out Kissinger for conversation and supper, insisting on speaking in German rather than English. Kraemer, a Lutheran, subsequently stated that he was taken with "this little Jewish refugee" he had seen, who "as yet knows nothing, but already he understands everything." Kraemer was Kissinger's first significant mentor and patron, assisting him to achieve distinction in the Army and get places and opportunities that would have been impossible to obtain on his own.

Kissinger never laughed about the day the Eighty-Fourth Division discovered the Ahlem detention camp on April 10, 1945. In reality, Kissinger did not mention the incident until long later, describing it as "one of the most horrifying experiences of my life." He recalled the detainees' "barely recognizable human" state and his "immediate instinct" to feed the starving men, only to realise that solid food killed several of them since they were unable to digest it. Kissinger was remembered by one surviving prisoner as the American GI who told him, "You are free." Kissinger soon after penned an essay titled "The Eternal Jew," which was a sarcastic homage to Nazi propaganda. "Who was lucky, the man who draws circles in the sand and mumbles, 'I am free,' or the bones that are interred in the hillside?" he pondered himself after the camp's liberation. When confronted with the camps, Kissinger conveyed a genuine emotion that many came to share: "This is humanity in the twentieth century."

Because Germany later developed as a peaceful democratic state, the American military government of Germany appears to historians considerably better than it does to contemporaneous observers. Left-wing critics complained about moderate denazification, which enabled too many former Nazis to remain in positions of authority, while right-wing detractors mocked the New Dealers, who intended to reform Germany but were unable to repair the economy. To many ordinary Germans, the initial postwar years were simply a period of hunger and suffering, during which cigarettes became common currency and the illicit market became a matter of life and death. In this chaotic situation, Kissinger proved efficient as commandant in Bensheim, despite the fact that he relied on some dubious Germans, including a police chief who was subsequently convicted of accepting bribes. Kissinger stayed in Bensheim until April 1946, when he accepted a position teaching at the European Command Intelligence School. The post was well-paying and permitted the "unmilitary" Kissinger to remain in Germany as a civilian. The post also reunited him with Fritz Kraemer, who was in charge of curriculum organisation. Kissinger, who was still only a high school graduate with some college courses in accounting and engineering, had the opportunity to lecture his former superiors on topics such as the structure of the Nazi state and German paramilitary organisations at the school, which was designed for officers serving in military government. As the political climate in Germany began to shift in late 1946, and the Cold War loomed, Kissinger expressed his own anti-communist opinions, demanding close supervision of German workers and a ban on Communists being employed at the school. Kissinger was also drawn to the school's academic environment, and among his outstanding peers were his future assistant Helmut "Hal" Sonnenfeldt and, subsequently, his Harvard colleague Henry Rosovsky. Kissinger also showed his rebellious side, refusing to submit a lesson plan for approval and breaking rules by keeping his dog in the barracks. "He was a problem person," the director of education later remembered, describing Kissinger frequently throughout his career.

Kissinger stayed in Oberammergau for a year before returning to the United States. Leonie Harbert, a colleague instructor and a German gentile, had become his lover. This generated conflict with his parents, who were concerned that he would marry her. He assured them that he was not in a "marrying or engaging mood," but his obvious loss of Orthodox Jewish faith added to their discontent. Kissinger defended himself and questioned their traditional ideas in multiple frank and often aggressive letters: "To me, there is not only right or wrong, but many shades in between." The true tragedies of life are not decisions between good and wrong... Real issues bear soul difficulties, causing agonies that you cannot grasp in your world of black and white." Many of the certainties that had guided Kissinger's life were broken by his wartime experiences, and he lashed out at his parents when they repeated them. His defiance surprised them, but he told them that he would adjust. "After all, not everybody came out of this war a psycho-neurotic."

When Kissinger intended to return to the United States to continue education, Fritz Kraemer warned him, "A gentleman does not go to the College of the City of New York," and advised him to leave "the city where your parents happen to be." Kissinger applied late, but Harvard accepted him, providing him a year's academic credit for his City College experience and one of the two Harvard National Scholarships awarded to New Yorkers that year. Kissinger returned to the United States, accompanied by his dog, Smokey, who had been dutifully transported by Harbert. Kissinger took the puppy to Cambridge in one of his ongoing minor rebellions, breaking Harvard rules but providing him with "a wonderful link between a life that was and one that will be."

Henry Kissinger who returned to Washington Heights in July 1947 was not the same man who had gone four years before. The Orthodox Jew from Fürth no longer practised Judaism, the refugee wielded power and authority over those who had rejected him, and the future accountant was about to enter America's most prestigious university. Other changes occurred as well, including alterations in Kissinger's perspective on the world and his beliefs about human nature and human beings. Kissinger's Army experience broadened and matured him, opening up new worlds, modifying his life expectations, and driving his indomitable drive. It also forced him to face the harsh truth of what happened to his family members who did not flee Germany. Kissinger's scathing judgement of human nature was expressed in a letter he wrote to the relatives of Helmut Reissner, a boyhood chum of Kissinger's in Fürth who had survived the extermination camps and was now on his way to America.

"WILD BILL" ELLIOTT AND HARVARD UNIVERSITY

Kissinger took Development of Constitutional Government in his first semester, taught by William Yandell Elliott, a Harvard Government Department legend who would become Kissinger's second great mentor. "Wild Bill" Elliott was not your average Harvard lecturer in the 1950s. He was a man of immense energy and dynamism, an athlete, poet, and scholar with what Kissinger called the "grand seigneur" manner. Others on the team were less impressed. Elliott was described as "slightly insane" by Stanley Hoffmann, and Daniel Ellsberg as "a terrible fake with a Southern accent." Elliott, a proud Tennessee native, served as an artillery commander in World War I and was an all-American football player for Vanderbilt University. He also had a brief association with the Fugitives, a renowned group of poets and literary scholars who met at Vanderbilt in the early 1920s to defend their view of the South and its agrarian way of life. Elliott received a life-changing Rhodes Scholarship and attended Balliol College at Oxford, where he learned to respect Oxford's individual tutorials, which he later applied with his Harvard students. In the 1930s, he was an outspoken opponent of the Neutrality Acts and advocate for intervention in Europe, a view that did not go down well on the Harvard campus. During WWII, he was the vice president of the War Production Board. After 1945, he frequently spent two to three days per week in Washington, DC, meeting with the House Foreign Affairs Committee.

Kissinger was not always cautious to distinguish his own ideas from those of Spengler and Toynbee, so some have interpreted Kissinger's dismal musings about America in the 1970s as a reflection of his susceptibility to Spenglerian historical pessimism. In truth, Kissinger opposed Spengler's and Toynbee's historical determinism, as well as their idea that history followed "laws" comparable to the natural world, which could be discovered by empirical inquiry. Kissinger was significantly more drawn to Kant's moral philosophy and its renowned "categorical imperative... the general formulation of which enjoins men to act in accordance with those maxims which can be made into a universal law." Kissinger, like Kant, believed that man had the ability to construct his own history. However, he did not draw Kant's upbeat implications from this assumption. In an eccentric reading of Kant, he contended that the German philosopher's work Perpetual Peace, which maintained that "mankind was progressing slowly but surely in the right direction" toward universal peace with a league of free republics, undercut Kant's own argument against determinism. Kissinger perceived a conflict "between Kant's moral philosophy and his philosophy of history." Reflecting on his own loss of religious faith, Kissinger rejected the idea of history having a transcendental meaning or purpose, and he questioned Kant's optimism about humanity's progress. Kissinger saw most of history as a tragic story, which Americans, with their hopeful national ideology, had difficulty comprehending and accepting. In the end, Kissinger's personal "philosophy of history" was "a curious amalgamation of ethical relativism and antimaterialism," according to historian Peter Dickson, in which "man must create his own meaning, values, and reality." This is described by Dickson as "Kissinger's existentialist philosophy of history."

The Korean War broke out only a few weeks after Kissinger graduated from college. Just as World War II altered his life and career ambitions, this new war in Asia provided new options. North Korea's June 1950 attack on the South was the Cold War's Pearl Harbor, convincing American officials that the Soviet Union intended worldwide dominance and triggering a mobilisation of the American state and its resources. America was now at odds with global communism. Following China's participation in November

1950, President Truman declared a national emergency, and worries of nuclear war intensified. Senator Joseph McCarthy's search for domestic communists heightened fears that America was facing both a foreign and a home danger. The Cold War had turned heated, and Henry Kissinger's life would be shaped by it for the next four decades.

Elliott made the case for two programs that Kissinger eventually directed, with the American government intensely worried about the ideological struggle and Harvard willing to collaborate. Kissinger took over the International Seminar program, which brought young leaders from Europe to Harvard for a six-week summer study. He anticipated that by giving "active, intelligent Europeans the opportunity to observe the deeper meaning of United States democracy," the program would promote Western solidarity.

Following the inaugural seminar in 1951, Elliott and Kissinger had the notion of creating a journal that would incorporate many of the seminar's ideas and discussions. Confluence was an attempt to "reach broader audiences in the form of something resembling an international forum." "In a world increasingly threatened by a pervasive orthodoxy, there must be room for free inquiry, discussion without polemic, and debate that assumes the good faith of all participants," Kissinger wrote in the journal. Using the editorial "we," Kissinger highlighted that "we are not neutralists," and that he disagreed with several of the authors. Later, some claimed that Confluence was a "false... principally an endeavour to make Henry known to outstanding individuals all around the world." That was certainly one outcome of the journal—it resulted in the first mention of Kissinger's name in The New York Times. However, it also mistook one outcome with the project's more laudable intentions. Confluence published an astonishing range of European thought, particularly German, and was widely disseminated in the new Federal Republic. It achieved significant notoriety for an academic journal, and it attracted prestigious authors and commentators in both the political and cultural realms, recruiting articles from figures like McGeorge Bundy, Reinhold Niebuhr, Hannah Arendt, Raymond Aron, André Malraux, Alberto Moravia, Enoch Powell, and Denis Healey.

Both the International Seminar and Confluence ran on tight budgets, and Kissinger spent a substantial amount of time trying to raise money. When Shepard Stone declined extra cash for Confluence in May 1954, Kissinger told him that it was "a bitter pill to swallow" and that Stone's argument for denying him funding was the equivalent "of committing suicide because of the fear of death." Confluence ran until 1958, when Kissinger opted to focus on the International Seminar. The CIA donated some money for both enterprises, eventually using several front organisations—including the Farfield Foundation and a group named the Friends of the Middle East—to make its donations. When this was discovered in 1967, along with the agency's support of Encounter and other important publications of the time, Kissinger denied knowing the true source of the money. While his denial is hard to accept, it is also the truth that the CIA's financing was exceedingly restricted. As Ferguson properly adds, "Kissinger's activities at Harvard were among the most staid operations of the cultural Cold War. In modern terminology, it was soft power at its softest."

In addition to the course and magazine, Elliott assisted Kissinger with his contacts in Washington, particularly the State Department's policy planning staff. Kissinger worked as a consultant for the Operations Research Office, which dispatched him to Korea in 1951. Kissinger also worked as a consultant for the Psychological Strategy Board (PSB), which funded his first journey back to Germany in May 1952. The spy agency itself was "a natural outgrowth and supplement to the operations of the CIA," and it was involved in the "ideological struggle for the hearts, minds, and souls of people around the world." Kissinger was also on the road as the head of the International Seminar, visiting with senior German officials and requesting feedback on US policies. In the Krupp armaments plant's dining room, the former refugee found himself the guest of a group of wealthy industrialists, some of whom had served the Nazi state. "Who would have thought," Kissinger said to his parents, that they would host a banquet in his honour. Along with recruiting future Seminar participants, Kissinger provided PSB with a report on German conditions. He had come not long after the US had signed the commercial agreements. The accords were intended to end the occupation system and hasten Germany's transformation into a Western ally in place of a peace treaty. These were followed by the signing of the treaty establishing the European Defense Community, the European military force to which Germany would contribute. The signing of the accords was attended by Secretary of State Dean Acheson, and the ceremony was hailed as a success for America's European strategy.

Kissinger, the young graduate student, had written a critique that was both insightful and self-serving within the wider Cold War consensus. It would mark the start of a distinct pattern in Kissinger's critiques and writings before he rose to power. The criticism would be negative, direct, and cogent, but it would rarely be tied to any one person or leader, and it would often be stated in a way that reflected his knowledge and sympathy for the policymaker's quandary. It would criticise tactics but never the fundamental principles behind Cold War containment policy. And would either highlight a project Kissinger was working on, back a political candidate Kissinger supported, or validate the wisdom of thoughts he had already expressed. As intriguing and perceptive as Kissinger's written works are, they should be viewed as largely utilitarian, aimed for political utility rather than intellectual coherence.

Kissinger worked on his doctoral dissertation while editing

Confluence, running the International Seminar, and advising for the government. He completed it in June 1954. The dissertation, titled "Peace, Legitimacy, and the Equilibrium (A Study of the Statesmanship of Castlereagh and Metternich)," was later published "almost unaltered" under the title A World Restored: Metternich, Castlereagh, and the Problems of Peace 1812-1822. The book examines the process of peacemaking performed by European diplomats following the Napoleonic Wars, which is an unusual choice of topic. According to John Stoessinger, one of Kissinger's graduate student colleagues, most of his contemporaries viewed history with mistrust and suspicion, feeling that "the past could not help us much to unlock the secrets of the future." Other graduate students jokingly inquired if Kissinger had heard of the atomic bomb. Kissinger stated that nuclear weapons did not render history obsolete and that it was important to examine a successful model of peacemaking, such as the Congress of Vienna. "I have chosen the period between 1812 and 1822 for my topic, partly, I am honest to say, because its problems seem analogous to those of our day," he said in the foreword. However, I am not a firm believer in this parallel. Even if denied, the significance of this period remains in the fact that it was confronted with the construction of a new international order, and thus with all the dilemmas of foreign policy in their most immediate form: the relationship between domestic and international legitimacy, the role of the balance of power, and the limits of statesmanship."

Kissinger needed a job after completing his doctorate. Elliott's influence in the Government Department was not enough to overcome some of the jealousy and hostility against Kissinger and his mentor, and he was not promoted to assistant professor right away. Kissinger continued his work on the International Seminar and Confluence as an instructor. Nonetheless, Kissinger was a man in a hurry, impatient with academic constraints, and immensely ambitious. He approached and obtained assistant professorship offers from both the University of Chicago and the University of Pennsylvania. Neither of them prompted Harvard to respond, but Kissinger was hesitant to leave Cambridge. He addressed a long letter of complaint to Harvard president McGeorge Bundy, lamenting the absence of "joy" in academic life, fiercely condemning the reliance on senior academics and the accompanying "conformity" and "mediocrity," and even expressing interest in law school.

THE PRESIDENTIAL CHANGE AND THE INSTALLATION OF THE NSC SYSTEM

When Richard Nixon invited Henry Kissinger to the Hotel Pierre in New York on November 25, 1968, it was only the second time the two men had met in person. The first time they met was at a Christmas party in 1967 at Clare Boothe Luce's house, where they had a brief discussion. Now the two men were having a long and rambling conversation about foreign policy, with Nixon voicing his disdain of the State Department and the CIA—Kissinger wrote on a yellow pad Nixon's frank "Influence of the State Department establishment must be reduced." For Nixon, stealing Nelson Rockefeller's prized academic adviser was a coup in and of itself, both in terms of reaching out to the liberal wing of his party and of besting Rockefeller, a frequent and fierce opponent. Nixon, although appreciating Kissinger's assistance in Vietnam throughout the campaign, wanted to ensure Kissinger's approval. Although the two men shared a professional interest in foreign policy and saw themselves as outsiders who were not fully embraced by the elites, they had very different temperaments and histories. Nixon came from a lower-middle-class, Quaker family in California, and he despised the Eastern Establishment, liberal Jews, and Ivy League intellectuals. Despite being in the most public of professions, he was a loner who despised confrontation with others and brooded over perceived and real slights. Kissinger was more outgoing than Nixon, loved dealing with the media and others with opposing viewpoints, and was self-assured of his intellectual superiority. They quickly became the odd pair of American politics, brought together by their mutual love of intrigue and power, as well as Kissinger's "tuning fork relationship with the president on the issues that mattered the most," as William Safire put it. Kissinger became more like Nixon in certain aspects, but was able to understand, anticipate, and, most importantly, control Nixon better than many who had known him for years. On November 27, 1968, Nixon invited Kissinger back to New York to meet with Nixon's campaign manager, and then his attorney general, John Mitchell, who asked him, "What have you decided about the National Security job?" When Kissinger replied that he had not been aware of the offer, Mitchell shouted, "Oh, Jesus Christ, he has screwed it up again." Mitchell, who had known Nixon long enough to recognize his indirect and non-confrontational manner, must have deduced that Nixon did not make the offer out of fear of Kissinger turning him down in person. Mitchell swiftly exited the room, telling Kissinger that the president-elect wanted to see him again. The offer was made this time, but Kissinger requested a week to "consult" with "friends and associates." It's difficult to believe Kissinger had any actual reservations about accepting the position, even though Ferguson believes he did have ongoing reservations about Nixon. He called Nixon's assistant Dwight Chapin on November 29 to accept the appointment.

During 1968, Kissinger was involved in a Harvard-based study that sought to recommend ways to facilitate a smooth presidential transition, and some of its ideas, particularly those concerning presidential control over foreign policy and the revitalization of the National Security Council (NSC), stemmed from this project. Kissinger argued that the arrangement he designed, which made the NSC—and Kissinger himself—the primary counsel to the president on international matters, was exactly what Nixon desired. The president believed that a more centralised and clandestine approach to foreign policy was required, and that the best way to do this was to transfer foreign policy decisions directly into the White House, as both Kennedy and Johnson had done. Kissinger underlined that Nixon would have been unlikely to allow him, as a Harvard and Rockefeller man, to put anything in place that did not adhere to Nixon's own tastes. While this is correct, it leaves out certain critical qualifications, namely Kissinger's own unique contribution to the new organisation and how it could benefit his own position. When Kissinger went to meet with Walt Rostow, President Johnson's equivalent of an assistant on national security concerns, Rostow instructed Kissinger that "the only right way to organise is to serve the President's needs." Kissinger took this advice to heart. With his weird recluse personality, great intelligence, and proclivity for deception, his NSC organisation served the interests of Richard Nixon. Nixon, like his great rival John F. Kennedy, and in stark contrast to his predecessor, Lyndon B. Johnson, believed that a president's primary responsibility should be foreign policy, saying once, "This country could run itself domestically without a President," and joking that domestic policy amounted to "building outhouses in Peoria." He had travelled widely as vice president and during his time out of government, and he was well-versed in various countries and their leaders. He was likewise persuaded of the significance of foreign policy on a president's domestic political position. His national security adviser, as the job was subsequently dubbed, was a presidential appointment who did not have to be confirmed by or appear before a Democratic Party-controlled Congress. Kissinger's constituency consisted of one man and one man only.

Bringing foreign policy inside the White House was Nixon's strategy of ensuring that the State Department did not obstruct the foreign policy innovation he sought—and claimed political credit for it. Kissinger was instrumental in this. When Nixon named his old buddy and Eisenhower's attorney general, William P. Rogers, as secretary of state, the press pondered whether Rogers, who had no experience in foreign affairs, could compete with Kissinger for the president's ear. Nixon and Kissinger, according to NSC worker and later Kissinger critic Roger Morris, carried out "a seizure of power unprecedented in modern American foreign policy," dubbed "the coup d'état at the Hotel Pierre." This coup had its limits, and it was not the triumphant capture of power over all foreign policy as Morris claimed. Secretary of Defense Melvin Laird obtained Nixon's approval prior to his appointment, giving him authority over his department. Laird's command of the bureaucracy and vast political relationships in Congress made him a formidable adversary to Kissinger.231 The Treasury Department likewise functioned independently of Kissinger, though the ramifications for foreign policy were not immediately evident. Despite being put at a disadvantage before the Nixon presidency began, Rogers' personal acquaintance with Nixon dated back to the Eisenhower years, and he had significant access to, and occasionally influence with, the president. Nixon sensed Kissinger's insecurity and used Rogers to exploit the national security adviser's weakness. Nixon, according to Kissinger, "did not really mind the tug-of-war that developed between Secretary of State Rogers and me," and was sure that "my special talents would flourish best under conditions of personal insecurity." He remarked that the best part of being national security adviser was that "you can be paranoid and have real enemies." In a more serious spirit, he said in his memoirs, "No one could survive the White House without Presidential goodwill, and Nixon's favour depended on his willingness to join the paranoid cult of the tough guy." The press conspiracy, the Establishment's enmity, and the Georgetown set's flatulence were permanent aspects of Nixon's talk, which could only be addressed at the expense of banishment from the inner circle." Kissinger wanted to be in the inner circle since January 20, 1969, and it would take his cerebral genius, courtier skill, and Machiavellian manipulation within and against the bureaucracy to keep him there.

Chapter 2: You Can't Lose All Of Them.

BE LIKE IKE: NIXON, THE FIRST HUNDRED DAYS, AND THE EISENHOWER ANALOGY

The first presidential inauguration to be met with irate demonstrators in Washington was Richard Nixon's. They organised a "counter-inaugural" and threw beer cans, rocks, and bottles at the procession. The Vietnam War-related public upheaval shaped American politics. Nixon declared, "We are entering an era of negotiation after a period of confrontation," and he begged Americans to "lower our voices" in a conciliation speech. The "cause of peace among nations" is something that Nixon pledged to uphold "sacredly," but he also issued a warning: "peace does not come through wishing for it—that there is no substitute for days and even years of patient and prolonged diplomacy." In contrast to John F. Kennedy's admonition to "pay any price, bear any burden," the Nixon administration's inaugural address heralded the start of a retreat strategy that would limit American obligations and shrink its influence overseas.

Nixon and Kissinger came to the conclusion that America's standing in the world had significantly shifted since the Kennedy administration. The United States appeared to be a prisoner of Gulliver across the world, caught up in wars it was unable to win and unable to break free from obligations it no longer desired. Vietnam ranked as the top priority, involving over 500,000 Americans in a bloody conflict that was killing over a thousand people every month. Many Americans were persuaded at home by the urban uprisings of the 1960s that the US could no longer pay its foreign obligations and the pricey weapons they demanded. Student demonstrations brought to expose the extreme polarisation and profound divides that exist in American society, along with the decline of the brash confidence of the Kennedy years. With its recent invasion of Czechoslovakia and border disputes with China demonstrating that it remained a formidable opponent, the Soviet Union now stood as an equal in nuclear weapons outside. While renewed violence seemed imminent in the Middle East, Western Europe was growingly consumed with its own internal issues and the desire for greater unity. The obstacles facing the United States seemed insurmountable.

Nixon and Kissinger understood the phrase to include the idea of credibility, both internationally and domestically, even if they couched the Vietnam commitment in terms of the national interest and used language of realism. According to Kissinger, none of the country's presidents could agree to Hans Morgenthau, a prominent realist, who demanded an abrupt and unilateral departure of American troops. Nixon thought that a quick pull out would result in a severe political problem in the United States, with Saigon probably collapsing and the North Vietnamese winning. It would be reasonable for critics to wonder, "What was the sacrifice of American blood and treasure for?" Why did my brother, father, or son have to pass away? Who was in charge of this mishap? Nixon felt that this would undermine his ability to lead. He agreed with Fritz Kraemer, Kissinger's mentor, who wrote, "The 'people' are not very just, they forgive the victor, but always make scapegoats of their own leaders who are not victorious," in a document that Kissinger delivered to the president.

Nixon and Kissinger's first aim was to put an end to the Vietnam War. Nixon employed a historical parallel and was aware that Americans had chosen him because they thought he would put an end to the Vietnam War. It was predicated on his perception of what transpired with the ascension of Dwight Eisenhower, Nixon's personal political hero and vice president. Nixon thought that Eisenhower had impliedly warned the Soviets that he would employ nuclear weapons in addition to all other options to put an end to the Korean War. Similar to Eisenhower, Nixon believed that an "honourable peace" that gave South Vietnam a "reasonable" chance to survive could be achieved through a combination of covert diplomacy with the Russians, threats of more forceful military action against North Vietnam, and promises of an arms control agreement and a Middle East settlement. Nixon understood that, despite the fact that many Americans had seen the Korean War's end as a "defeat" in 1953, Eisenhower had been able to focus on other matters that were more crucial at the time, such as setting up NATO and calming the McCarthy backlash against internal communism. Likewise, Nixon aimed to quell domestic antiwar demonstrations and reestablish American dominance over European allies. Nixon believed that the best outcome the United States could hope for in South Vietnam would be something akin to the Korean War.

Kissinger's commendation was similar to the criticism he had frequently written about American leaders' interactions with Europe, but this counsel would soon run against the reality that Europe was becoming more inward-looking and unresponsive to a revival of American leadership in the mould of Eisenhower from the 1950s. Within the next fifteen months, every European leader Nixon had seen had disappeared; de Gaulle's retirement in April 1969 served as a precursor to this shift. As Nixon and Kissinger initiated their strategy towards the Soviet Union, it became evident that Nixon truly limited international consultation. Kissinger acknowledged to Rogers over the phone that Nixon "is not so much for consultation in practice as in theory." Nixon knew that the American public valued his leadership of the alliance, but he soon turned his attention away from Europe and toward Vietnam and the Soviet Union. Nixon thought that the Soviet Union may be persuaded to utilise its clout with Hanoi to terminate the Vietnam War by a new strategic weapons accord.

Kissinger agreed with Nixon that the United States should prioritise finishing the Vietnam War expeditiously, notwithstanding his personal links to Europe. Nixon gave Kissinger the go-ahead to serve as his confidential envoy in a series of secret "back channel" meetings with Soviet ambassador Anatoly Dobrynin in order to engage the Soviet Union. Nixon told Soviet leaders that the United States was "determined to end the war in Vietnam one way or another" in the early days of Kissinger's administration. In addition, Kissinger explained his linkage theory to Dobrynin by stating that Soviet support for bringing the war to an end would lead to advancements on other fronts, such as the Middle East and the strategic weapons talks.

Nixon felt he needed a military option to show the North Vietnamese and the Soviets that he was serious, particularly after the North launched its post-Tet offensive in February 1969, which ended a lull in the fighting and resulted in the deaths of over a thousand American soldiers in a short period of time. After spending a large portion of his public career arguing that "our insistence on divorcing force from diplomacy caused our power to lack purpose and our negotiations to lack force," Kissinger agreed with him. Kissinger put pressure on the armed forces to propose options that "may demonstrate to the North that a new, strong hand is at the wheel." Despite Nixon's desire to attack the North, Rogers and Laird informed him that a resumption of bombing North Vietnam could rekindle domestic unrest and jeopardise the president's early honeymoon with the American people. Alternatively, B-52 strikes against enemy locations and havens inside Cambodia were suggested by General Creighton Abrams. Although the United States had approved covert operations against some of the sanctuaries, no large-scale operations had been carried out, and the North Vietnamese had acquired control of substantial portions of eastern Cambodia, in violation of that nation's neutrality. If combined with an offer of secret discussions with the North Vietnamese, Kissinger contended that such a military action—oddly code-named Breakfast—"will serve as a signal to the Soviets of the Administration's determination to end the war." Invoking Nixon's often-stated "madman" strategy—

that is, his reputation for anti-communist fanaticism might serve to scare both the Russians and the North Vietnamese into believing that he might escalate even further and thus into making concessions—Kissinger continued, saying that it would also "be a signal that things may get out of hand." On March 16, Nixon gave his approval for the bombing, which Haldeman recorded the following day in his diary as "Historic Day." At 2:00 pm our time, K[issinger]'s Operation Breakfast was finally launched. Both K[issinger] and P[resident] were ecstatic. The leader of Cambodia, Prince Norodom Sihanouk, was helpless to stop the Americans from bombing his country or the North Vietnamese from occupying it, so he chose not to publicly criticize the bombings.

The purpose of the covert bombardment of Cambodia was to keep "domestic critics" from using the incident as justification for resuming their criticism of the war and putting "pressure for a quick US withdrawal" on the American people.36 Both the North Vietnamese and the Cambodians knew about it, and if they disclosed the information, there were backup plans to say it was an error. Nixon and Kissinger proceeded to approach the Soviet Union directly, ostensibly threatening to use further force against North Vietnam, when the North Vietnamese made no protests. Kissinger summoned Dobrynin to his house late on April 14, 1969, in a scene straight out of a Hollywood screenplay. He informed the ambassador that the meeting was so private that "he gave the maid the evening off and set the tea table himself." In addition, Putin instructed the Secret Service to investigate if any reporters had followed Dobrynin home or were simply loitering outside. "The President had therefore decided to make one more direct approach on the highest level before drawing the conclusion that the war could only be ended by unilateral means," Kissinger declared in a dramatic manner to the Soviet envoy. Kissinger also offered a clear-cut domestic political explanation for Nixon's reasoning and motivation in Dobrynin's account of the meeting, stating that Nixon "is not seeking a military victory, but he cannot go down in American history as the first U.S. president to have lost a war in which the U.S. participated." Kissinger clarified that Nixon thought Hanoi was depending on a breakdown in US resolve following growing demonstrations. Kissinger, however, informed Dobrynin that Hanoi was mistaken and that "ending the war as soon as possible by any means, if necessary by using even greater military force" was backed by the American people, who included both Nixon supporters and "the more than 12 million who voted for Wallace." If, on the other hand, "the war in its current form is prolonged for an additional three years until the next election, electoral defeat is inevitable." Kissinger emphasised that relations with the Soviet Union were at a critical turning point and even gave Dobrynin the president's signed approval of his talking points for the session. They would be able to advance on a number of topics, such as arms control and the Middle East, with a settlement in Vietnam. In order to negotiate a settlement, the talking points also mentioned the idea of sending a "high level representative" to Moscow to meet with a representative from North Vietnam. (Kissinger intended to send Cyrus Vance, the former deputy secretary of defence.) Nixon, according to Kissinger's conclusion, "will be assured of winning the next election, since at least 80 percent of the electorate will vote for him" if he was successful in mending his relations with the Soviet Union.

Dwight Eisenhower passed away on March 28, 1969, two weeks prior to the Korean crisis. When Nixon learned of the development, he unexpectedly started crying in front of Kissinger, Haldeman, and Rogers, among other members of his staff. Nixon remarked, "He was such a strong man." Nixon intended to take Eisenhower's lead from the outset of his presidency. But the North Korean response demonstrated that Nixon did not inherit the world from the thirty-fourth president. After Eisenhower was elected president, the United States no longer possessed the overwhelming military and economic might it possessed. In the Korean War, Eisenhower did not face a single, cohesive Communist nation. The Sino-Soviet split was becoming dangerously violent as evidenced by the first major military conflict between the Soviet Union and China in the northeastern border region early in March 1969. America's influence was limited, the world had changed, and Nixon needed a fresh strategy.

VIETNAMIZATION, "SALTED PEANUTS," AND THE MAKING OF A WASHINGTON CELEBRITY

Kissinger had hoped that the Soviet leadership would respond to his request for Ambassador Dobrynin to set up covert discussions and break the impasse in Vietnam. Rather, the Vietnamese Communists presented a ten-point peace plan on May 8, 1969, calling for the complete departure of American forces and the establishment of a new coalition government in Saigon. Nixon felt compelled to react. Kissinger drafted a fourteen-point plan that called for both sides to withdraw their forces within a year under international supervision after informing Haldeman that Hanoi "may be folding." The formula, which was similar to the original Geneva arrangements from 1954, called for the international supervisors to ensure that elections were held in South Vietnam. Nixon stressed that even if reports from Hanoi suggested it was depending on a "collapse of American will in the United States... there could be no greater error in judgement," remarks that Kissinger hoped would be helpful in potential peace negotiations. However, Nixon also said that he could not expect Americans, "whose hopes for peace have too often been raised and cruelly dashed over the last four years," to show "unlimited patience."

Melvin Laird, the secretary of defence, was intimately aware of the shifting public sentiment. Vietnamization, or preparing the South Vietnamese army to over combat duties from the United States, was Laird's program of choice for disengaging from the conflict, and he soon rose to prominence within the administration. Having served on appropriations, foreign policy, and intelligence committees for sixteen years, Laird had extensive experience of Capitol Hill and was able to discern the threat posed by the growing popularity of antiwar and anti-defense spending sentiments. Insofar as practicable, he aimed to maintain the Defense Department's budget for the three main missions of Europe's defence, containment, and nuclear balance with the Soviet Union. Laird's Vietnamization strategy succeeded in bringing the troops home, buying the government some time, and avoiding the need for cooperation from the Soviet Union and North Vietnam. Nixon announced the first troop withdrawal of twenty-five thousand personnel at his June 1969 meeting with President Nguyễn Văn Thiệu on Midway Island, realising the political benefits of Vietnamization. Just a few days later, during a news conference, Nixon became enraged when asked about former defence secretary Clark Clifford's demand that all ground combat soldiers be removed by the end of 1970. "I would hope we could beat Mr. Clifford's timetable, just as I think we have done a little better than he did when he was in charge of our national defence," Nixon said, pointing out how Clifford's own tenure as defence secretary had corresponded with high casualties and an increasing number of troops in Vietnam.

Haldeman said that Nixon's remarks "shook Kissinger pretty badly." Kissinger saw Nixon's last-minute attempt to surpass Clifford's proposal as detrimental to any chance of reaching an agreement with Hanoi for reciprocal withdrawals. He fretted that this indicated the president no longer trusted him and conjectured to Haldeman that this would lead to the fall of the Saigon government. Although Haldeman believed Kissinger was exaggerating, Kissinger's uncertainty was part of a bigger picture. It was no secret that Nixon and his close advisors mistrusted many of the people Kissinger had brought to Washington who were not supporters of the president. When the Times published the Beecher story about the bombing in Cambodia, Kissinger himself erupted in fury. Nixon detested press leaks, and Kissinger and the men he brought with him were the main suspects in the climate of mistrust that pervaded the White House. Kissinger "set out to prove to Nixon and his Prussian staffers that he was more fervent than anyone in enforcing the cult of secrecy" in response to the White House's concerns and to protect his personal reputation. Kissinger threatened to "destroy whoever did this if we can find him, no matter where he is" when he called FBI director J. Edgar Hoover, providing him with a list of employees in his office who had access to the material. The NSC system's co-creator Morton Halperin, fellow German Jewish exile Helmut Sonnenfeldt, and even Kissinger's "conscience" on foreign policy matters, Winston Lord, were among the first people to be wiretapped. All told, the White House had ordered seventeen FBI wiretaps; thirteen targeted government workers, including Kissinger's staff, and four targeted journalists, including the columnist Joseph Kraft, the journalist Hedrick Smith of the New York Times, and Kissinger's British friend Henry Brandon, a reporter for the London Times. The wiretapping highlights Kissinger's positional instability and fragility within the Nixon White House, as well as his resolute efforts to utilise all means necessary to maintain his close relationship with the president.

Under Kissinger's guidance, the NSC was to devise a "savage, punishing blow" that would demolish a large portion of the North in a brief campaign. While many military options were considered for Duck Hook, such as using tactical nuclear weapons, destroying the dikes that prevented the Red River from flooding, or even launching a ground invasion of the country, the most likely course of action was to launch a heavy bombing campaign that would "attack 29 significant targets in North Vietnam... and aerial mining of the deep water ports." "He wants to push for some escalation—enough to get us a reasonable bargain for a settlement within six months," Haldeman said of Kissinger. Kissinger made an effort to get Nixon ready for the escalation during the summer of 1969. Nixon needed to make a "total mental commitment and be prepared to take the heat" that would accompany the planned military strike, he told Haldeman and Ehrlichman.

The antiwar movement's announcement of plans for a large mobilisation and demonstrations in Washington, which would start on October 15 and continue every month until the war was finished, was the most significant gauge of the public's mood. The goal of the "moratorium" movement was to normalise protest in the lives of middle-class Americans. On September 16, 1969, Nixon declared that another 35,000 American troops would be leaving Vietnam, along with intentions to reduce the draft by 50,000 men in the next months. Taking into consideration the possibility of unrest on campuses, the actions were implemented before the start of the autumn term of college. "The President hopes that this combination of troop withdrawal and draft suspensions will give him a longer spell of freedom from domestic confrontation," hypothesised newspaper columnists. Legislation was presented by Republican senator Charles Goodell of New York to impose a deadline of the end of 1970 for the withdrawal of American forces from Vietnam.

Nixon attempted to remain flexible as the deadline for Operation Duck Hook drew closer, expressing optimism for a new phase of peace and diplomacy one moment and informing Republican senators that he was thinking of a plan to invade North Vietnam and blockade Haiphong Harbor the next. He assured them that he would not be "the first American president to lose a war" and that "by the 1970 elections, one way or another, it is going to be over with." Nixon was truly conflicted; he understood Hanoi's approach of waiting him out but did not want to incite the domestic protest movement with an unproven military escalation. Kissinger and Nixon both believed that good diplomacy required the use of force. He searched for excuses to put things off, once conjecturing with Kissinger that the North's stubbornness could be attributed to Ho Chi Minh's passing in September. Observing the president's indecisiveness, Kissinger provided him with additional justifications to delay going to war. Nixon asked Kissinger if he could make "the tough move" before October 15 in order to avoid appearing to have been impacted by "the rioting at home," following a press conference in which he made it clear that he would not be affected by the domestic protests planned for October. Kissinger advised against it, stating that Hanoi should be allowed until November 1 and that there was a "ten percent chance Hanoi might want to move."

Nixon admitted to Haldeman that he realised support for the war was becoming "more tenuous every day" as the date drew near. He was angry with Laird and Rogers for warning him repeatedly that a military build-up would destroy the nation and ruin his presidency. Kissinger informed the president that he preferred escalation and that he believed there were only two options: "to bug out or accelerate." As Kissinger posed it to Nixon, the primary concern was whether he could keep the nation together for the roughly six months required for this plan to be effective. Haldeman, who had a lot of sympathy for Kissinger on the matter, believed that Kissinger had misjudged the degree of civilian opposition to any military build-up, even if it meant winning the war. Kissinger's "contingency plans," in his opinion, "did not include the domestic factor." Nixon was convinced by Kissinger's proposal that his national security adviser was aware of his gut feeling, even though the president would have made a different decision in this instance. Nixon made the decision in early October to forgo a military attack on November 1. Nixon had to make a difficult choice since it went against his perception of himself as a leader who was not scared to defy the public opinion surveys. Kissinger was also concerned that Nixon might be trying to ease him out and that he had lost faith in him. However, Nixon wanted to try a bluff, taking a chance on his hypothesis of the "madman" to see if he might advance a settlement. He and Kissinger conspired to call him while Kissinger was having a meeting with Dobrynin, the Soviet envoy. Nixon stressed throughout the call that the Soviet Union "should not expect any special treatment until Vietnam was solved" and that "Vietnam was the critical issue." Additionally, Nixon had Kissinger inform Dobrynin that "the train had just left the station and was now heading down the track" and that it was a "pity that all our efforts to negotiate had failed." Despite the sinister sense of threat these statements were meant to evoke, Dobrynin appeared unfazed. Just that "it was an aeroplane and not a train and could leave some manoeuvring room" was all he said to Kissinger.

Nixon and Kissinger erroneously believed that Moscow would be willing and able to exert influence over Hanoi. North Vietnam was a point of contention between the Chinese and Russians for influence, and the country's leaders were deftly manoeuvred for their personal gain by the North Vietnamese. Historian Ilya V. Gaiduk came to the conclusion that although the Soviet Union had given Hanoi almost half a billion dollars in aid by 1969, "not converted into proportional political influence." Though they grumbled, Soviet officials were never prepared to condition their assistance on behavioural changes in North Vietnam. Furthermore, despite their complaints about Vietnamese "intransigence," the Soviets supported North Vietnam throughout the war, hoping that it would be crucial to their long-term ambitions for influence in Southeast Asia. Vietnam was "not only an issue of ideology but also a question of geopolitics," as Gaiduk put it, to the Kremlin.

Nixon launched his own counteroffensive against the peace movement and the moratoriums on November 3 in his well-known "Silent Majority" address. Kissinger gave the speech's main ideas, but Nixon added "rhetorical flourishes throughout," in his own words. Nixon made the argument that "a nation cannot remain great if it betrays its allies and lets down its friends" in support of the war. Nixon made an appeal to the "great silent majority of my fellow Americans" to help him end the war "in a way that could win the peace" in the speech's most well-known passage. "North Vietnam cannot defeat or humiliate the United States; only Americans can do that," Nixon stated icily. In addition to Vice President Agnew's remarks against the media, the administration's offensive produced instant results in surveys of public sentiment. Nixon was thrilled, as Kissinger, a perceptive observer, noted, "when foreign policy was used for domestic political purposes." Despite his professed indifference to public praise, he enjoyed the few instances of recognition that he received. Popularity for the president surged into the upper 60s and 70s, and the administration's "dual-track strategy of Vietnamization and negotiations" gained widespread support, according to Kissinger. The intensity of antiwar protest started to wane even as the Vietnam moratorium in mid-November brought fresh protests to Washington. The November moratorium was not as well covered by television news, with a lot of attention now going to counter-demonstrators and "silent majority" organisations. There were no noteworthy protests in December. "Pretty thoroughly got into the position of calming down the war opposition, killing the mobilizations, and assuring the people he's got a plan and that it's working," was how Haldeman described the president's actions. "The Administration had some manoeuvring room for the first time since January," Kissinger wrote in his conclusion.

Henry Kissinger's position was rife with irony as the first year of the Nixon administration came to an end. In order to end the Vietnam War, Kissinger had counselled the president to seek cooperation with the Soviet Union on arms control and to establish a deadline for military action against North Vietnam. Ultimately, Nixon withdrew his ultimatum against Hanoi, and the US restarted the Strategic Arms Limitation Talks (SALT) without attaching any strings. Even though his advice was mostly ineffective, Kissinger became the most well-known public figure in Washington during the Nixon administration, showing up in society pages and news columns alike. One of the most well-known anecdotes about Kissinger was written by Maxine Cheshire, a society columnist for the Washington Post, who frequently wrote about his comings and goings. Kissinger was carrying a manila envelope with the stamp "The White House " on it when he came late to the party at the home of Washington socialite Barbara Howar. When someone asked Kissinger how he "never put the packet down all evening, not to eat or to drink or to talk," he replied in jest, "It's my advance copy of Playboy." Kissinger responded, "Well you couldn't call me a swinger because of my job," to a statement made by Sally Quinn, a fellow Washington Post reporter, who said, "Oh so you're really a swinger underneath it all." How about you just pretend that I'm a swinger in secret? The term "secret swinger" gained popularity. Kissinger relished the attention, despite reporters making fun of his new title. "Are you the famous White House swinger?" called columnist Rowland Evans. "Jesus Christ!" cried Kissinger. I'm done with the additional tasks. Evans continued, telling him that he would never live up to the title. In response, Kissinger said, "I just hope that everyone will remember that I am an Arizona State teacher."

Kissinger's jest about getting lost in an Ivy League university far from home encapsulated the self-deprecating humour that won over detractors. "The appearance of power is therefore almost as important as the reality of it; in fact, the appearance is frequently its essential reality," Kissinger realised in the context of Washington culture. Kissinger continued to brief the media only on an anonymous "background" basis, but this "appearance of power" was enhanced because reporters were aware of his close ties to the president. Kissinger purposefully sought attention from the media, spending hours on the phone with reporters outlining the administration's policies and emphasising his crucial influence over it. Kissinger devoted "at least 35 percent of his time and energy on press matters," according to one aide, and 50 percent, according to another. When speaking with reporters, Kissinger could be deliberately evasive in order to project the impression of a "dove" or restraint among Nixon's inner circle. After having his phone tapped, liberal journalist Joseph Kraft, who maintained a cordial relationship with Kissinger, stated subsequently, "Kissinger tries to come on as the secret good guy of the Nixon foreign policy Establishment." Actually, on the majority of significant international business, he seeks to support and legitimise the President's rigid impulses. A few weeks following the revelation of the "secret swinger," Cheshire called Kissinger to inquire if the astronauts of Apollo 12 had been asked to carry one of his female friend's earrings to the moon. "For God's sake no," Kissinger virtually roared in response. But while they spoke, Cheshire informed him that she frequently received calls from readers reporting sightings of Kissinger, saying, "People are more interested in you than President Nixon." A few months later, Kissinger represented the administration at Lenin's 100th birthday celebration at the Soviet embassy. Surrounded by international diplomats, Kissinger relished his image as a "ladies' man" and was described as "the centre of attention." "I was much more resistant two years ago, before I got this reputation as a swinger," he added. It's awesome to be irresistible right now.

KISSINGER AND THE "NEW REALISM" OF AMERICAN FOREIGN POLICY

Early in January 1970, Richard Nixon sent a warning to his staff, citing the possibility that this would be the "worst year" of his administration given the fact that the United States was experiencing its first recession in nearly nine years. They would just have to "ride it through," hoping that 1971 and 1972 would bring better times. Nixon thought that his foreign policy, with a potential summit with the Soviets and progress toward ending the Vietnam War, would be one of the year's highlights. Nixon desired coordination and control from the White House, which Kissinger would continue to supply. However, there would be repercussions to the administration's general layoffs.

Over the course of the following several months, the United States found itself effectively led by its ally, in spite of internal concerns, regular forecasts of failure, and persistent pleas for intervention from Germany's political opposition. The movement toward European détente happened far faster than Kissinger and Nixon had hoped thanks to Brandt's determination to follow paths recommended by previous U.S. administrations. These included talks with Moscow, exchanges with East Germany, and recognition of the Oder-Neisse border with Poland, which was established after World War II. Following the Soviet invasion of Czechoslovakia in August 1968, the European détente movement—which French President Charles de Gaulle had spearheaded earlier in the 1960s—seemed to come to a standstill. Although Brandt revitalised it, Kissinger was concerned that Brandt's actions might reignite a "debate about Germany's basic position" in the West, "not only inflaming German domestic affairs but generating suspicions among Germany's western associates as to its reliability as a partner" because of his complicated and personal history with Germany. "[Brandt's] problem is to control a process which, if it results in failure could jeopardise their political lives and if it succeeds could create a momentum that may shake Germany's domestic stability and unhinge its international position," he concluded in a memo to Nixon of that same nature. Kissinger was more comfortable with the stability of Germany remaining divided than with resuming the effort for German reunification, particularly if it meant severing Germany's links to the West. However, as a result of the "new era in international relations" that Kissinger himself had heralded, the United States was powerless to rein in Brandt.

Kissinger met with the North Vietnamese in secret three times in the following two months. "If we can hold here in the United States for two to four months... we'll have it," he said to Haldeman following their second meeting. Kissinger tried to persuade the North Vietnamese that they would benefit from a negotiated settlement with the US. Kissinger claimed to be "a professor on leave," and he was informed that the North Vietnamese believed he was playing a prank on them. Kissinger said, "But we are not trying to do so—not because it would be in our interest, but rather because we are not particularly benevolent." In a geography lesson with obvious implications, Kissinger noted that Hanoi "would be closer to South Vietnam than we... [and that] we want a settlement which is in their interest" following a settlement. Kissinger said that President Nixon had substantial backing from Americans in an effort to refute Hanoi's assessment of the strength of the peace movement. "The international situation has complications which may make Vietnam no longer the undivided concern of other countries and may mean that Vietnam will not enjoy the undivided support of countries which now support it," he said, making a reference to the Sino-Soviet confrontation. He joked that "Harvard professors always speak for 55 minutes" as he wrapped off his speech. "North Vietnamese smiles" was noted as the response in the transcript, but the explanation was left out.

Kissinger tried to build a personal rapport with the resolute revolutionaries on the Vietnamese side by using charm, self-deprecating humour, and even an allusion to his rising stardom. He joked, "If I leave on Sunday, everyone will think I have a girl," as he tried to work out a date for their next meeting with the North Vietnamese. After the initial meeting, Kissinger informed Nixon that, in his opinion, the atmosphere was "remarkably frank and free of trivia," and that "it was certainly the most important [meeting] since the beginning of your administration and even since the beginning of the talks in 1968." The most challenging issue for Kissinger, meanwhile, came from the Communist demand that the United States take action to remove the "military agents, people like Thiệu, Ky, Khiem," prior to any kind of deal. It was the result that interested the North Vietnamese, not the method Kissinger recommended. "Our proposals are realistic, reflect reality, and align with the aspirations of the South Vietnamese people," stated their negotiator, Lê Đức Thọ. Only by using these techniques will the political relationships in South Vietnam be accurately reflected and registered in a political process. The inflexibility of the North Vietnamese stance suggests that Kissinger's hope for a negotiated resolution sprang solely on his role as the negotiator.

Nixon's decision to send American forces into Cambodia in April 1970 put Kissinger's commitment to a negotiated settlement to the test as well as his relationship with the president. The pro-American defence minister, General Lon Nol, had taken the Nixon administration by surprise last month when he successfully spearheaded an overthrow of Prince Norodom Sihanouk. Despite the covert bombing, ties between the US and Cambodia improved. Sihanouk even praised the Nixon Doctrine and made what Kissinger described as "an unabashed pitch for aid" after full diplomatic contacts were restored. Nixon gave Kissinger instructions to ask the CIA "to develop and implement a plan for maximum assistance to pro-U.S. elements in Cambodia" as soon as word of the coup reached Washington. He also told Kissinger to treat the situation like "our air strikes," that is, behind closed doors from the bureaucracy. Nixon chose to wait in response to protests from Rogers and Laird that supporting Lon Nol so quickly would validate rumours that the US was orchestrating the coup. However, as soon as it was evident that the new Cambodian government was adopting a strong anti-North Vietnamese position, covert support started. Nixon was especially happy when Hanoi's supply of forces in the South was halted by the new government's closure of the port of Sihanoukville.

Attacks by the North Vietnamese in Cambodia quickly escalated, raising major concerns about the survival of the Lon Nol administration. Following his alliance with the communist Khmer Rouge, North Vietnam declared its support for Prince Sihanouk's ascent to power. Nixon and Kissinger were now thinking about attacking the North Vietnamese refugee camps in Cambodia. Similar to Operation Duck Hook, Laird and Rogers opposed the notion of deploying any American military in Cambodia due to their primary concerns about the domestic political ramifications. According to Laird, the Army of the Republic of Vietnam (ARVN), which is made up of South Vietnamese forces, could complete the task on its own and would not cause as much internal turmoil as an American campaign would. Kissinger continued to doubt the ARVN's ability to carry out an operation of this magnitude. As chair of the Washington Special Action Group (WSAG), he oversaw operations to provide military support to the Cambodians after realising that Nixon planned to assist Lon Nol. (The National Security Council subcommittee on crisis management, known as WSAG, was established following North Korea's downing of an American spy plane in April 1969.) He also believed that Hanoi might be forced to engage in real negotiations if a military campaign altered the situation on the ground.

During these covert discussions over Cambodia, Nixon made a significant TV announcement on April 20, 1970, saying he would remove 150,000 troops from Vietnam over the course of the following year. The news of troop withdrawals sparked a heated internal dispute that culminated in this. Kissinger really liked the higher figure over the more often disclosed smaller withdrawals, despite his reservations about the approach. He justified it by saying that it would preserve American bargaining leverage and provide the military the leeway to maintain additional combat forces in Vietnam until the very end of the deadline. The issue was that the president's address, which had a significantly larger number than anticipated, encouraged people to believe that the war was coming to an end. Nixon applauded Americans for their "steadiness and stamina," which would enable the achievement of a "just peace" in Vietnam, and hailed the departure announcement as evidence of the program's success. The primary message of Nixon's address was that he was, in fact, ending the Vietnam War by troop withdrawals, despite the fact that it also included cautions about communist gains in Laos and Cambodia. The psychological climate in the nation that heightened shock and indignation at the decision to invade Cambodia was influenced by Nixon's speech.

Though he was preoccupied with bolstering his own personal standing with the president and the bureaucratic struggle with Rogers and Laird, Kissinger may have warned Nixon of the peril of this approach. "Do you think there is a prayer for Vietnamization if Cambodia is taken over?" he asked Rogers as he carried on their argument. By going straight to William Westmoreland, the interim head of the Joint Chiefs of Staff, Kissinger assisted Nixon in keeping Laird and Rogers out of some of the most important discussions and secured military backing for the move. "Can understand the political people thinking of reasons why we shouldn't," the president clarified, "but the military usually stands with the Commander-in-Chief and he wants to do something." "I hope you need a political analyst in the army," Kissinger joked as he concluded the talk, acknowledging Westmoreland's offer of assistance. I will always be unable to return to Harvard. It's possible that he was responding nervously to criticism he was receiving from his own NSC employees through his humour. Among other things, three of his closest advisors, Roger Morris, Winston Lord, and Anthony Lake, forewarned their boss that "U.S. troops in Cambodia would have a strong and damaging political effect in the U.S., which would both hurt the President's Vietnam policies and divide the country further."

Nixon declared on April 30, 1970, that the United States would deploy troops to Cambodia. Nixon aimed to emulate the triumph of his November 3 "Silent Majority" address, rousing his followers "with the bark on—patriotic, angry, stick-with-me-or-else, alternately pious and strident," working with his most bellicose speechwriter, Pat Buchanan. Kissinger and Haldeman both cheered and said, "It will work," noting that it was a "very strong and excellent wrap-up," when he read the speech to them. Nixon made a startling announcement that North Vietnam was stepping up its "military aggression" in Cambodia and that this was endangering "the lives of Americans that are in Vietnam now." He then made up a lie, or as Kissinger put it, "a sentence that was as irrelevant to his central thesis as it was untrue," claiming that the US had "scrupulously" maintained the Cambodian people's right to neutrality while disregarding both covert actions and the B-52 bombardment. Nixon created the impression that American GIs were assaulting a communist Pentagon by emphasising that the American attack was aimed at the "headquarters for the entire communist military operation in South Vietnam," or COSVN, when outlining the steps that America would now pursue. As for how the Cambodian incursion may expedite Vietnamization and bring an end to US involvement in the war, Nixon did present a more convincing argument. Reminding Americans, he said, "We have halted the bombing of North Vietnam." We've reduced air operations by more than 20%. We have declared the departure of more than 250,000 soldiers. We've made the offer to remove every man we have if they remove theirs. "If, when the chips are down, the world's most powerful nation, the United States of America, acts like a pitiful, helpless giant, the forces of totalitarianism and anarchy will threaten free nations and institutions throughout the world," the president then chose to use Churchillian rhetoric. It was a stark contrast to what he had said just ten days before, upending the nation's equilibrium and confronting his adversaries. Nixon "had done what only Nixon could do," as Safire put it in a sympathetic note, "making a courageous decision and wrapping it in a pious and divisive speech."

Even former Harvard colleagues who had worked in government during the Kennedy-Johnson years, such as Richard Neustadt, Francis Bator, and Adam Yarmolinsky, squared off against Kissinger. Kissinger offered to discuss policy with his "close colleagues and friends" in private, but they declined. They had made up their minds to publicly oppose administration policies. Ernest May, a historian, made the most incisive and instructive remark to

Kissinger when he said, "You're tearing the country apart domestically," adding that this "would have long-term consequences for foreign policy as tomorrow's foreign policy is based on today's domestic situation." According to Thomas Schelling, an economist, Kissinger had two options: The president either didn't realise he was invading another nation when he entered Cambodia, or he did understand. We just cannot decide which is scarier. Kissinger, Schelling said later, "sat in pained silence, and just listened." Kissinger "behaved with great grace and dignity and courage under intense emotional pressure from his peer group," according to Francis Bator, President Johnson's NSC portfolio holder for Europe.

But Kissinger went on to criticise the professors' "lack of compassion, the overweening righteousness," and the exaggeration that dogged many of their remarks. He was most likely the source of the reports that surfaced claiming the Harvard group had threatened to deny him entry again after his government service. The "meeting completed my transition from the academic world to the world of affairs," according to Kissinger. His relationship with Richard Nixon, who respected his loyalty but despised his suffering, was further enhanced by this. A few weeks after the Cambodian decision, during a brief vacation in Key Biscayne, Florida, Nixon invited Kissinger, Haldeman, and Ehrlichman to his Air Force One cabin, telling them that since they had absorbed the majority of the criticism in the preceding weeks, they should be honoured with an award similar to the Purple Heart. He then gave them the "Blue Heart," a hand-sewn blue cloth heart created by Nixon's close friend Bebe Rebozo's partner for those who were "true blue." A month later, Kissinger's office was relocated from the White House basement to the West Wing, which is conveniently close to the Oval Office, where it was much larger and more opulent. This resulted in a new moniker that was inspired by a well-known play: "Playboy of the Western Wing."

The Middle East situation worsened as the clamour over Cambodia started to wane. In 1969, Nixon and Kissinger had not paid much attention to the Middle East. Kissinger did make a comparison between the current state of affairs with the Balkans prior to 1914, a region in which the activities of minor but ferocious allies may push the great powers into war. Israel was a good fit because it had nuclear weapons by now. As one of the few peoples whose survival is truly threatened, Kissinger forewarned Nixon that "the Israelis are probably more likely than any other country to actually use their nuclear weapons." Nixon advocated for the Israelis to adopt a policy of "nuclear ambiguity" and refrain from introducing or testing nuclear weapons in the region during his initial discussions with Israeli Prime Minister Golda Meir in September 1969. Nixon thought that Kissinger's Jewish heritage prevented him from having an unbiased view of Israel, which is why he officially delegated responsibility for the Middle East to Rogers. But he also urged Kissinger to speak with Soviet envoy Dobrynin about issues related to the Middle East. Along with this, Kissinger established his own back-channel relationship with Israeli envoy Yitzhak Rabin, via which he received information not available to the State Department. Conflict was inevitable because of this. The Rogers Plan, a comprehensive framework to bring peace to the region through an Israeli departure from occupied regions in exchange for an end to hostilities and diplomatic recognition, was revealed by Rogers in December 1969. As the president who was most detached from the "Jewish lobby," Nixon was keen to establish lines of communication with the Arab world in order to pull it away from the Soviet yoke. When French President Georges Pompidou and his wife were beaten by American Jewish protests in Chicago in February 1970, Nixon became enraged and postponed selling the Jewish state the state's cutting-edge Phantom jets. Nixon also ordered Kissinger to alert the Soviets to the "gravest concern" on their planned deployment of "combat personnel in the Middle East." The alert was issued far too late. The Soviets had already made the decision to deploy thousands of troops, pilots, and surface-to-air missiles (SAMs) to Egypt in order to assist in defending against Israeli deep-penetration air strikes. Dobrynin gave the Kremlin the assurance that Americans would be reluctant to take strong action against such a Soviet initiative because they were concerned about "a new Vietnam" in the Middle East.

Kissinger should take the lead in White House relations with Russia since Nixon still wanted to maintain control over them. "You should regard everything Kissinger says as coming personally from me," he said to Dobrynin, an extraordinary endorsement in Dobrynin's experience. Kissinger "positively glowed with pleasure and from the acknowledgment of his importance," according to Dobrynin's notes. But Kissinger had long harboured grave doubts about the State Department's Middle East initiatives, stating to Haldeman in March that the region will "blow up" and that "I have not believed in what we are doing in the Middle East for ten months." Kissinger thought that the Soviets had a "blank check" for their new military presence in Egypt thanks to Rogers's attempts to broker a cease-fire, a move that would "enhance [Soviet] geopolitical influence." At the end of June, Kissinger told reporters at a background briefing that the US was "trying to expel the Soviet military presence" from the Middle East. This statement infuriated the State Department. An irate Kissinger responded, "Sometimes I give up," to a call from New York Times columnist Max Frankel asking if he had been "expelled" from the California White House. Are you asking us to declare that we support Soviet influence in the Middle East? "The SOB is trying to prove that everything the White House has done since January 20, 1969, has been wrong and he is trying to save the country," Kissinger vehemently protested about Rogers, fearing—correctly—that his own standing with the president had soured. Kissinger became much more identified with the Israelis as a result of his bitterness toward Rogers. His battle with Rogers, he said William Safire, was "like the Arabs and the Israelis." He'll win the war, but I'll win every battle. He just needs to defeat me once.

AUTUMN OF CRISES IN KISSINGER: CHILE, CUBA, AND JORDAN

Henry Kissinger described the three weeks in September 1970 when "three major crises descended upon the administration in corners of the world thousands of miles apart" in his memoirs in a foreboding manner. "They all represented—or seemed to us to represent—different facets of a global Communist challenge," he asserted, even though he acknowledged that the "causes of these events were fundamentally different." Kissinger may have known that later writers would break down the three problems and condemn the administration for believing they were all connected to the Soviet Union, which is why he included the term "seemed to us." This brief era was not viewed by many of its contemporaries as especially terrifying or crisis-filled. But every crisis exposed Kissinger's flaws and virtues as a presidential advisor, revealing both his caution and his hubris. Significantly, these crises altered the nature of his battle with Secretary of State Rogers, highlighting Kissinger's significance to Nixon and solidifying his standing as the second most powerful person in the White House.

The most spectacular crisis occurred in the Middle East when the extremist Popular Front for the Liberation of Palestine (PFLP) took control of three planes headed for Jordan and kept the occupants captive in the desert while being watched by television crews and reporters from around the world. After the hostages were freed, the planes were blasted apart in a display of dramatic explosions that served as a terrifying visual representation of the possible perils in the Middle East. These incidents were a part of a wider power struggle in Jordan, when Yasser Arafat's Palestine Liberation Organization (PLO) and the PFLP both posed threats to King Hussein, the moderate. Nixon and Kissinger perceived the war from the first as being instigated by a Soviet Union eager to assist its radical partners in overthrowing the pro-Western Hussein. "It appears that the Soviets are pushing the Syrians and the Syrians are pushing the Palestinians," Kissinger said to Nixon. There isn't much reason to press the Palestinians.

During the Cold War, Kissinger viewed Israeli dominance in the area as a tactical advantage. In contrast to Rogers, who supported a "slow and measured escalation" and was prepared to wait to see whether the Syrians pushed farther than northern Jordan, Kissinger supported a tough message to the Soviets, direct action by the Israelis, and a complete Syrian withdrawal when Syrian tanks rumbled into Jordan. Rogers was more concerned about the Soviet reaction and how any Israeli ground actions would affect the prospects for peace. Rogers felt that Kissinger was pressuring the president to make a snap judgement and that he wanted to maintain some distance between the US and Israel. Kissinger was successful in persuading Nixon to back an Israeli strike, but he was reassured when the Soviet Union promised to take action to contain Syria. The WSAG met multiple times over the course of a twenty-four-hour period beginning late on September 20, discussing and assessing the reports of the Syrian invasion and Jordanian counterattack. Awaiting further developments, they considered King Hussein's proposal for airstrikes against the Syrians.

The Syrian action was actually a part of an internal power struggle in Damascus, and General Hafez al-Assad, the head of the Syrian air force, declined to employ air cover to stop his rivals' tank invasion. Assad quickly became the victor of the conflict. The Syrians fled after the Jordanian air force destroyed nearly one hundred of their tanks. The Palestinians had been vanquished by King Hussein, and it's possible that Israeli and American threats had contributed to this outcome. Yitzhak Rabin, the Israeli ambassador, contacted Nixon, stating that the following factors contributed to the successful outcome: "first, the tough U.S. position; second, the Israeli threat; third, Russian pressure on Syria and Iraq as a result of the U.S.

position; fourth, superb fighting by Jordanian troops." Nixon told Haldeman this information. Later that day, Kissinger said to Nixon, "I think we are over the hump of this one."

Even if Kissinger exploited the crisis to further his personal agenda in his conflict with Rogers, there may still be a legitimate national security concern. The American charge is supported by the declassified diplomatic correspondence between Kissinger and Soviet envoy Dobrynin, particularly the Russian documents themselves. The idea that the Soviets might test this understanding by basing submarines armed with nuclear weapons in Cuba was not implausible. The "understanding" that ended the Cuban Missile Crisis—the Soviets removed their missiles in exchange for a promise that the United States would not invade Cuba—remained ambiguous. Kissinger's assertion that the Soviets were contesting the "understanding" that ended the Cuban Missile Crisis did neither surprise nor infuriate Dobrynin. American surveillance aircraft discovered that the Soviet Union was constructing infrastructure on Cienfuegos Bay. This information revealed SAM sites, communication towers, barracks, and other establishments that might be utilised for submarine maintenance. It is scarcely unreasonable to question whether Kissinger was wondering whether this was part of "a process of testing under way in different parts of the world" during the height of the Soviet challenge in the Middle East.

The Nixon administration handled the problem in a low-key manner. During their subsequent encounter, Kissinger was informed by the Soviet envoy that although the Soviet government upheld the 1962 agreement, there were some "clarifying questions" regarding the definition of a base. Their "base" would have to host ships "carrying offensive weapons; i.e., submarines or surface ships armed with nuclear capable, surface to surface missiles," according to a series of conditions provided by the Americans. The Soviets upheld their end of the bargain notwithstanding the sporadic protests. Feeling tremendous satisfaction from their accomplishment, Kissinger suggested to Nixon that it would not be detrimental to "tell a few of those Senators who we gave a briefing the bare essence of the thing." "This was done with minimum humiliation for the Soviets," Kissinger said to a reporter. Kissinger retorted angrily, "That's not true," to the reporter's statement that agreements between Washington and Moscow were the foundation for both the resolution of the Middle East crisis and the Cuba issue. It would be great if it were. An agreement with the Russians is the only thing we would want. Anyone who has lived through the previous 25 years understands that conflict yields no victory.

Kissinger felt that the results of his work in Cuba and the Middle East had shown Nixon how valuable he was and how crucial his covert conduit to Dobrynin was. He was certain that the administration's display of power, prudence, and moderation would establish a standard for interactions with the Soviet authorities that would enable the "understanding" that Kissinger desired. But the third crisis that accompanied Kissinger's fall raises a different question about the viability of his diplomatic initiatives. Salvador Allende, a Marxist Socialist who was running for president of Chile in partnership with the Communist Party of Chile, emerged victorious on September 4, 1970, taking home 36.6 percent of the vote. Since Allende was close to both the Soviet Union and Fidel Castro, the Communist world hailed his win as a historic setback to American imperialism. "Chile voted calmly to have a Marxist-Leninist state, the first nation in the world to make this choice freely and knowingly," the American ambassador in Chile, Edward Korry, wrote to Washington. Exaggerated anxieties were stoked in Washington since this defeat happened in the region of the world that is so frequently referred to as the United States' "backyard."

Regarding his career, one of the most contentious issues is still Kissinger's role in Chile. Prior to assuming his role as national security adviser, Kis-singer had little interest in the continent of South America. Kissinger was cited as saying, "Nothing important can come from the South," and "What happens in the South has no importance," during a 1969 discussion with the foreign minister of Chile. Kissinger acknowledged the minister's assertion that he had no knowledge of Latin America and said, "You're right." Furthermore, I don't give a damn. Prior to September 1970, Kissinger minimised Chile's importance and disregarded it. "Chile was a dagger aimed at the heart of Antarctica," he jokingly said. In addition, he said to his colleagues, "I don't see why we have to let a country go Marxist just because its people are irresponsible," with a mixture of cynicism, black humour, and arrogance.

Kissinger played to Nixon's emotions, but he also recognized them. Nixon did not want "a Cuba in his administration," keeping in mind the events of the recent past. Kissinger realised right away that Chile offered him another chance to demonstrate to Nixon how crucial his command of foreign policy was to him. Representing the consensus within the State Department, Ambassador Korry bemoaned the "grievous defeat" that the United States had experienced. However, he thought that any attempt by the United States to support a coup would be "to court a failure as massive and damaging to American interests as the Bay of Pigs." As the president persisted and the State Department was hesitant to step in, Kissinger took on the position with resolve, motivated as much by a desire to strengthen his bond with Nixon as by a deep-seated worry about the threats Chile posed. Kissinger informed Secretary of State Rogers that "the President's view is to do the maximum possible to prevent an Allende takeover, but through Chilean sources and with a low posture" in response to his warning not to do anything in Chile that would "backfire" on the United States.

In his capacity as the head of the "40 Committee," which was responsible for overseeing American covert operations, Kissinger facilitated the passage of Track I, a bill intended to persuade the Chilean Congress not to choose Allende. After this strategy failed, Kissinger assisted in launching Track II, which involved locating generals in Chile who would carry out a coup in order to stop the Congress from selecting Allende. Tragedy was inevitable, with American intelligence operatives eager to get things done quickly and willing to spend big money. "It assumed too much reliability from people over whom we had no control," a subsequent critic observed. In its hunt for willing generals, the CIA came upon retired Gen. Roberto Viaux, a far-right extremist who had no friends in the Chilean armed forces. In addition, some of the anti-Allende forces that the CIA agents in Santiago were in contact with were preparing to abduct General René Schneider, the head of Chile's armed forces and a fierce opponent of any meddling in the political process. A week before the Congress of Chile was to gather in mid-October, Kissinger called Nixon to inform him that the Track II attempt "looks hopeless" and that he had "turned it off." An unsuccessful coup would be the worst thing possible. In response, Nixon reaffirmed the need for a "coolly detached" approach to Allende and demanded that the US stop providing financial support to the Allende administration. Kissinger promptly concurred as Nixon continued, calling this the "worst diplomatic mess" the US had ever found itself in.

Kissinger had carried out his president's orders to force an unyielding American bureaucracy to adopt a strict policy toward Chile. The "contagion" of the Chilean example was the two men's main concern. Kissinger confirmed that the effect of Allende's Marxist anti-American policy would extend to Europe, as Nixon stated: "If [Allende] can prove he can set up a Marxist anti-American policy, others will do the same thing." Kissinger did not stay closely involved in Chilean affairs, but the US made a major attempt to topple Allende during the course of the following three years. Opposition political parties received over $3.5 million, newspapers and other media received about $2 million, and business, labour, and other organisations received $1.5 million. Additionally, the US orchestrated a "credit squeeze," which made the financial issues facing the Allende administration worse. Despite all of these steps taken and the realisation that the American policy was an overreaction to the danger that Chile's socialist experiment posed, Kissinger is given too much credit or blame for events that happened in Chile that he had no control over.

VIETNAM, THE MIDTERM ELECTIONS, AND KISSINGER'S ASCENDANCY

Nixon concluded his own analysis of the "autumn of crises" with a statement that was eerily similar to Kissinger's: "Communist leaders believe in Lenin's precept: Using bayonets, probe. If you come across mush, keep going; if you come across steel, back off. Even though we were unable to stop Allende from taking over, at least in Jordan and Cuba in 1970, their investigation had revealed clear steel. Even though Nixon and Kissinger valued these displays of power, they both understood that the American people's primary foreign policy concern could still be summed up in a single word: Vietnam. As the midterm elections drew near, Nixon wanted to show that he was making headway toward ending the war and turning into a "peacemaker." American casualties had dropped significantly after Cambodia, and the intensity of fighting had abruptly decreased. There was a growing momentum within the US government for cease-fire proposals. In an attempt to be a major player in these discussions, Kissinger travelled twice to Paris in September 1970 for meetings with the North Vietnamese in secret. Kissinger proposed a 12-month plan for troop withdrawals, but he insisted that the US would not consent to the South Vietnamese government being overthrown by force. A "political process that would offer opportunities for each side to achieve whatever popular support it could muster" was Kissinger's attempt to woo the North Vietnamese, but he insisted that "we could not in advance guarantee to such or such a party that it would win and we should both agree to respect the outcome." Kissinger believed that the goal of Hanoi was to "eradicate organised non-Communist opposition." After that, they can unite with the disorganised non-Communists, who have no chance of surviving in such conditions. Kissinger "seemed to be sad, thinking that no result could be secured at this forum," the North Vietnamese recorded, citing Hanoi's previous positions as simply restated by the North Vietnamese and their rigidity. However, Kissinger acknowledged that although there were significant political divides between the US and North Vietnam, these differences "are small enough so that everything else can be settled" when it came to the military.

Nixon attempted to link anti war protester disruptions to broader voter anxieties about crime and disorder, even though the Vietnam War would prove to be less significant in the midterm elections than the rise in unemployment and ongoing inflation. Nixon informed his advisors that "permissiveness is the key theme," and the Republican campaigns focused on the "social issue," attempting to link Democrats to the alleged "anarchy" of the time. While Kissinger made an effort to avoid the campaign trail, Nixon saw fit to utilise him in the California Senate race, where Republican senator George Murphy was up against a formidable opponent in John Tunney, a close friend of Ted Kennedy's and the son of a well-known boxer. Kissinger refused, stating to campaign director Robert Finch that he detested "being used in the Jewish community." Kissinger retorted, "But they are all Jewish," in response to Finch's statement that the briefing was for "friends of the president." After Finch pledged to include a few gentlemen, Kissinger concluded, "If [Nixon] wants me to do it, I will." "The one group I hate to talk to is a Jewish group," Kissinger insisted, even after bragging to a reporter that his event had raised more money than the Murphy campaign had ever raised in California.

When Kissinger was first speaking with journalist Marilyn Berger early on Election Day, November 3, 1970, he asked, "What are you taking me away from, a Republican landslide?" "I can't see it," he said in response to her question about his seriousness. The midterm elections were a disappointment to the Nixon White House, intensifying Nixon's fear that he would be a one-term president. Nixon could take some comfort in the defeat of a few of his adversaries in the Senate, such as Charles Goodell in New York, Joseph Tydings in Maryland, and Albert Gore, Sr., in Tennessee. However, most of the candidates the president campaigned for lost, including Murphy in California and George H. W. Bush in Texas. The Republican attempt to capitalise on a violent protest against Nixon in San Jose, California, had backfired. Republicans did gain two seats in the Senate but lost nine House seats and eleven governorships—the overall Democratic margin in House elections increased from 1.1 million votes in 1968 to 4.5 million in 1970.

Nixon was shaken by the results. His own popularity was slipping below 50 percent, and he was angry when a Gallup poll showed that Americans thought the country's prestige abroad had fallen during his presidency. "We are not getting credit for foreign policy," he angrily told Haldeman. In a long memorandum in early December, Nixon told Haldeman he wanted a meeting with special counsel Dick Moore, speechwriter Safire, and Kissinger. Nixon had "reluctantly concluded that our entire effort on the public relations front has been misdirected and ineffective." What was needed in Nixon's view was "to get across those fundamental decencies and virtues which the great majority of Americans like—hard work, warmth, kindness, consideration for others, willingness to take the heat and not to pass the buck and, above all, a man who always does what he thinks is right, regardless of the consequences." Nixon knew Haldeman might wonder about including Kissinger in this group, but Nixon was direct: "The reason is that he will love sitting in such a meeting. He will keep it absolutely confidential; he will not contribute anything on how to get the ideas across, but above everything else, he is our big gun in the area where we have had our greatest success, and while he does not know it, he is the one who has been measured as the favourite."

The connection between the domestic politics of foreign policy and Kissinger's ascendancy is also suggested by Haldeman's detailed record of the almost-daily Kissinger-Rogers struggle. Early in the fall, Nixon was still concerned about the ongoing rivalry between the two men, telling Haldeman that he would have to "get them both to quit acting like little children, trying to nail the other and prove him wrong." Nixon agreed with Haldeman that it might be good to suggest to Kissinger that he think of leaving, if only "to shake him a little." If one had to go, it would probably be Kissinger, and Nixon then said he would put Kissinger's deputy, Al Haig, into his position. Only two months later the positions of Rogers and Kissinger were reversed. Haldeman complained to Nixon about Rogers's disloyalty to the administration, and Nixon asked him to put together a documented case against the secretary of state. Haldeman suspected Nixon wanted a case for the removal of Rogers, though he knew how difficult it would be for Nixon to fire his old friend. Nixon recognized how important success in foreign policy, and getting the credit for that success, would be for his reelection. The best bet for those political benefits was Kissinger. He was now, as Haldeman told Kissinger, "indispensable to the President, and both he and the President know it, and he's got to stay here."

By this point Kissinger had become the consummate courtier, recognizing Nixon's desperate need for praise, especially after his televised speeches and press conferences. He could almost read Nixon's mind in talking about political figures, aware of the president's resentments and manipulating his grievances. After his October 1970 cease-fire speech, Kissinger called Nixon to tell him it went very well, and that Senator Charles Percy, a leading dove, called him to say that it was "a brilliant speech, one of his finest ever." Before conveying that sentiment, Kissinger, knowing Nixon's mixed feelings, remarked, "That son of a bitch Percy called," and when Nixon asked whether he should call him, Kissinger replied, "I hate to see an opportunist rewarded." After a courteous conversation with his former staff member Anthony Lake, who had now joined up with Muskie's campaign, Kissinger called Nixon and told him of his conversation with that "snake Lake." Nixon also loved the flattery Kissinger provided. When Kissinger called after a press conference in December, Nixon asked him to tell his daughter Tricia his reaction. "I thought your father was spectacular," Kissinger said. "This was by far the best press conference he has ever held." A sceptical Tricia asked him why it was "the best," and Kissinger explained that it was because her father was "conciliatory and tough." Even after Nixon got back on the phone, he continued to tell Tricia all of Kissinger's various compliments. The next month, after another press conference, Kissinger told Nixon that the British journalist Henry Brandon had told him that Nixon was better at press conferences than Kennedy was, "more articulate and more disciplined." Nixon replied, "Really? That's like talking against Christ."

Kissinger's ascendancy owed much to his bureaucratic manoeuvring, his skill with the media, and his relationship with Nixon. It also stemmed from his ability to discuss foreign policy in new ways, and his language of retrenchment and realism was perfectly coordinated with the political mood of the nation. In year-end briefings for the press, Kissinger used the language of realism to discuss foreign policy. "It is really our interests that should get us involved, not our commitments." America needed a debate "on what and where are our interests, and only then should we look at our commitments." Kissinger understood the real limits of American power. He told the journalists of his occasional frustration that "one of the great dangers with trying to deal with such a high number of issues and problems is that the urgent ones seem to displace the more important ones." Kissinger noted, "It is a constant fight to find time to address those questions which have long range implications." As Nixon entered the second half of his first term, he and Kissinger attempted to deal with those long-range issues, hoping to complete a significant change in American foreign policy that would reverberate domestically and win the president reelection in 1972.

Chapter 3: Peace Is Really at Hand

At 11:00 a.m. Eastern Standard Time on January 24, 1973, all three television networks paused their regular programming to host a briefing given by Henry Kissinger. The famous quote from Kissinger that ABC's Howard K. Smith used to tell his viewers that "peace is really at hand now" was mentioned. Smith, noting that this announcement would be the "remarkable climax of a remarkable diplomatic year for Henry Kissinger," which included the trip to China, the SALT agreement with the Soviet Union, and now the peace treaty ending the Vietnam War, made up for Kissinger's usual tardiness. Although Time magazine, a historic establishment institution, had named both Kissinger and Nixon its "Men of the Year," these accomplishments were also those of President Nixon.

The settlement and Kissinger were the main topics of discussion on all three networks that evening. White House footage of his signing the accords with the North Vietnamese in Paris was shown, followed by a summary of his extensive news conference. They emphasised Kissinger's promise that American detainees would be freed two weeks after the deal was formally signed. Kissinger's briefing was referred to as a "typical Kissinger seminar" by Marvin Kalb on CBS because it was "long, articulate, and occasionally vague." Nixon and Kissinger had completed their diplomatic "trifecta" with the signing of the Paris Peace Accords: peace in Vietnam, SALT, and China. Richard Nixon won an overwhelming reelection, largely due to the effectiveness of the American foreign policy that Kissinger had come to represent. Kissinger was instrumental in the planning and formulation of the "realist" revolution in American foreign policy during this crucial election year of 1972, which was intended to have the greatest possible impact on domestic politics at home. Kissinger's new global "structure of peace" and the domestic power struggle were key to the "trifecta."

CHINA, THE EASTER OFFENSIVE, AND THE MOSCOW SUMMIT

Nixon experienced a temporary surge in the polls following his January 25, 1972, speech on Vietnam, in which he disclosed Kissinger's covert negotiations with the North Vietnamese. For a while, at least, Vietnam was not the big political topic, even with the ongoing primary races. Nixon and Kissinger were concerned that a military push by North Vietnam would lessen the political impact of Nixon's impending visit to China. Nixon felt that any attack may be connected to the Vietnamese Lunar New Year and turn into another Tet Offensive, therefore he approved a series of bombing operations in early February to attempt and avert any potential attack. As the "Harrisburg Seven" were finally put on trial, Kissinger himself continued to be somewhat visible in the media about a Vietnam-related matter. The trial ultimately embarrassed the Justice Department and the FBI. It garnered extensive media coverage and continued into April. The case resulted in a mistrial on the most serious allegations, including the attempt to kidnap Kissinger, because the jury did not trust an informant.

Kissinger learned that the North Vietnamese intended to meet with him in secret in mid-March as the departure for China drew near. The national security adviser informed Nixon he was "ecstatic" and that he was positive this meant there wouldn't be a big offensive and that there might even be a "breakthrough" in the negotiations. Nixon was strongly questioned about this by a sceptical party who thought the negotiations might be just another Vietnamese ruse. Nixon went so far as to say that the US's involvement in Vietnam was a "mistake," "because the way it's been conducted has cost us too much compared with what it would cost us to let it go." Nonetheless, the two men acknowledged that they would not have been able to leave Vietnam in 1969. As a "demonstration of strength," their resolve in Vietnam had prompted the China tour, according to Kissinger.

Kissinger argued, "We gained a helluva lot more from the secret meetings than they did," in support of his negotiation efforts. Even yet, he expressed optimism for a breakthrough and hinted at a reasonable break: "I think we can find a solution if they are willing to maintain a non-Communist structure in the south for a while."

Nixon, who had prepared mentally for the trip to an extreme degree, said to Kissinger as they were wrapping up their talk, "I'm a little more Chinese than many Americans." Nixon was talking about his upbringing in California and his time spent in school with Chinese students, but he also convinced Kissinger that the two of them were the only ones who truly grasped the importance of the trip, as opposed to "Connally or Agnew or Rogers." The two men did, in fact, become closer on their journey to China. To their mutual advantage, Nixon and Kissinger enjoyed the covert and scheming manner in which they executed their diplomatic coup, despite the fact that they were capable of being fiercely envious and small-time rivals. As the press corps jokingly referred to it, "Nixon's primary," it was crucial to Nixon's reelection campaign. For Kissinger, it was a pivotal moment in his rise to prominence in Washington, placing him second only to William P. Rogers and the State Department.

The China tour was largely centred around television coverage, which served as a political tool by highlighting Richard Nixon's role as well as the symbolism of the reconciliation of erstwhile foes. Kissinger compares the "obsessive single-mindedness of the advance men" who accompanied him on his planning trips to China to previous "barbarians" that the Chinese had dealt with, displaying a snobbish scorn for them in his memoirs. "We don't want [the Chinese] thinking we're using the summit for political purposes," he remarked, fretting over their obtrusive presence. Nixon was more concerned with China's significance to the American people than he was with any of Kissinger's philosophising about the country. Nixon's staff made great efforts to communicate that this would be a "journey for peace." China provided a unique benefit for American television coverage: events in the early evening could be aired live on American morning shows, and news stories about the morning might feature the evening news. To guarantee maximum publicity, Nixon's advance team—headed by Dwight Chapin but overseen by Haldeman—carefully planned activities. They coordinated the scheduling of Mrs. Nixon's visits to schools and communal farms, the welcoming feast, Nixon's visit to the Great Wall, and Nixon's arrival and departure to coincide with prime viewing hours for television coverage. "Nixon was finally getting the kind of 'p.r.' he had sought for more than three years," critics said. According to a Gallup poll, 84% of people approved of Nixon's travel to China, and 98 percent of respondents were aware of the visit—a record at the time.

Nixon was overjoyed with the trip's outcome and enjoyed both the public's and establishment media' accolades (James Reston's New York Times story on the visit was titled "Mr. Nixon's Finest Hour"). Nixon instructed Haldeman to call his buddy Bebe Rebozo in Key Biscayne and "have him give Henry all of his phone numbers of girls that are not over thirty." Nixon also commended Kissinger's work throughout the trip, especially the communiqué. When Kissinger reported that he had received strong backing from Ronald Reagan after his phone call, he was especially happy. Reagan understood the politics surrounding Nixon's trip, in contrast to other conservatives like William Buckley of the National Review. But Nixon also soon realised that he needed to emphasise more how the president was "a big league operator" and that this was a "classic battle between a couple of heavyweights" and that Kissinger was not doing enough to boost Nixon's image. He persisted in pressuring Haldeman and Kissinger to devise strategies for showcasing the trip's accomplishments. However, Nixon turned down Marvin Kalb's request for Kissinger to appear on television. "We have to be concerned about his proclivity to build himself as the power behind the throne," he said to Haldeman. Perhaps there is just no changing him.

As he took on the task of organising the president's visit to Moscow, Kissinger thought the US had escaped fate. He believed that the likelihood of a big offensive had decreased, even if the North Vietnamese had cancelled their scheduled meeting with him for March. He maintained that Hanoi was isolated as a result of its "triangular diplomacy" with the Russians and Chinese, and that its authorities would attempt to resolve the issue before the election in November. He also cautioned Nixon against granting General Abrams's fresh requests for significant airstrikes into North Vietnam in an attempt to thwart a potential offensive, for fear of inciting domestic political unrest and jeopardising ties with China. Kissinger was concerned that an October onslaught by the communists, just before the presidential election, might occur. "It's a hell of a gamble for them to take, because if they don't tip you over in October, then they've had it," he reassured Nixon, nonetheless.

But North Vietnam chose to take a chance well in advance of October. The Vietnamese politburo, headed by Lê Duẩn and Lê Đức Thọ, was encouraged by its forces' performance in Laos and thought they could win the war outright. Prior to the start of the offensive, Lê Duẩn, the top member of the North Vietnamese politburo, warned the Chinese that Hanoi would not put up with another "betrayal" similar to what had happened at the Geneva Conference in July 1954 and accused Zhou Enlai of sparing a "drowning" Nixon by granting him a successful visit. Because they wished to maintain positive ties with the United States, the North Vietnamese were afraid that pressure from their Chinese and Soviet friends might come again to accept the division of their nation. Nixon's concern for his new alliances with China and the Soviet Union, according to proponents of the attack within the politburo, would prevent him from retaliating. Additionally, they thought that the US presidential election and antiwar public sentiment would stop Nixon from escalating the war. However, several members of the Politburo advised caution, stating that Nixon is a very bold person who might take that risk, regardless of the repercussions. We must not undervalue him.

During the "Easter Offensive" on March 30, 1972, hundreds of North Vietnamese forces crossed the demilitarised zone with the intention of taking Hue, the imperial city, and Quang Tri, the provincial seat. They were armed with Chinese and Soviet tanks. Additionally, there were military assaults in two other areas of South Vietnam: the Central Highlands, where there was a threat to split the nation and take Kontum, and the Tay Ninh region, which is close to Saigon, where An Loc was also under threat. These were conventional military assaults, carried out by regular North Vietnamese soldiers, unlike the Tet Offensive of 1968. They surrounded Quang Tri and drove out South Vietnamese forces in the DMZ, where they first found success. The offensive was broadcast on US television as well. Reports from the evening news revealed wounded South Vietnamese soldiers and civilians escaping the conflict. "So far the results are not encouraging," CBS correspondent Bob Simon said, reiterating the administration's claim that the offensive would be a test of Vietnamization. Nixon retorted, "Well, we knew that yesterday," as soon as Kissinger entered his office on Monday morning, April 3, stating, "It is clear there's a massive attack."

Kissinger moved swiftly to put Nixon's policies into effect in the days following the attack by North Vietnam. Kissinger was at the centre of both military and diplomatic decision-making because of his tremendous stamina and energy, as well as his virtually unrestricted access to Nixon. Without delay, he exerted pressure on Admiral Moorer to increase American strength in the area. He even set up a meeting between Nixon and General John Vogt, sending the latter to take charge of the air campaign in Saigon. Additionally, he supported Nixon in his dealings with General Abrams in Saigon and Defense Secretary Laird, both of whom Nixon believed were not acting aggressively or imaginatively enough in their response to the attack. Nixon and Kissinger's efforts brought "to bear firepower beyond anything" the North Vietnamese had anticipated: six aircraft carriers, five cruisers, forty destroyers, and over one thousand warplanes, including over 150 B-52s. However, there would be significant tension with the military. Regarding diplomacy, Kissinger informed Nixon that he would urge the Russians to intervene with Hanoi by using his back channel to Ambassador Dobrynin. He proposed, with Nixon's enthusiastic support, threatening to use US power with the West Germans to stop them from approving their treaties with the Soviet Union and even from allowing Willy Brandt's government to continue, which the Soviets had developed significant ties with. Kissinger reportedly told Nixon that Dobrynin was "slobbering" for him to make a covert travel to Moscow in order to arrange the summit, and that this indicated the Russians were probably getting ready to "screw" their friend, North Vietnam.

Although Nixon was more dubious of Russian policy than Kissinger was, he nonetheless appreciated Kissinger's aid. Nixon also believed Kissinger was motivated by the potential for fame and publicity that came with leading another covert operation to Moscow. Nixon noted in his notebook that, "despite all of his many virtues, Henry does seem too often to be concerned about preparing the way for negotiations with the Soviets," adding that Kissinger appeared to think that "we can survive politically" even if the United States failed in Vietnam. That being said, Nixon "had no illusions whatsoever on that score." Not only would the United States lack "a credible foreign policy," but Nixon realised that losing the Vietnam War would also mean his chances of winning reelection would be slim to none. He informed Kissinger that since he would obviously be unable to run for reelection, he was thinking of cancelling the summit, imposing a blockade on North Vietnam, and searching "for a successor." Sensing that Nixon merely needed confirmation that he was vital to the nation, an emotional Kissinger turned down the proposal. Nixon made it clear that Vietnam had to be Kissinger's top focus in Moscow if he was to be granted permission to visit. Nixon had threatened to call off the summit amid the Indo-Pakistani crisis, and Kissinger thought he may reconsider. Kissinger was itching to visit Moscow. He used political scheming to control the president by informing Nixon that a liberal columnist named Joseph Kraft, who was "violently opposed to everything we're doing," had suggested that the US should "knock off the summit," and that this was irrefutable proof that "the Democrats" would prefer for the summit to fail. Nixon gave down and permitted Kissinger to travel to Moscow, but he stressed that Vietnam should come first. He said to Kissinger, "I'm willing to throw myself on the sword," at a dramatic moment. We will not allow this small asshole of a country to defeat this one."

In the wee hours of April 20, Kissinger surreptitiously departed Washington, bringing the Soviet envoy Dobrynin on Air Force One. Nixon's misgivings about Kissinger's intentions and motives had not gone away; he feared that Kissinger would spend "hours and hours and hours on philosophical bullshit," meaning that the meeting would never get to Vietnam. Nixon sent another lengthy memo, criticising Kissinger's briefing book and emphasising once more, "Your primary interest, in fact your indispensable interest, will be to get them to talk about Vietnam," even before the flight arrived in Moscow. He wasn't entirely off. Kissinger was very friendly when he first met with the leaders of the Soviet Union, against Nixon's orders and confident in his own negotiating approach. In the hopes that Nixon would follow through on his inauguration's declarations and transition from a "era of confrontation to an era of negotiation," he allowed Soviet leader Leonid Brezhnev to steer their first discussion. When Kissinger was able to finally shift the conversation to Vietnam, he contextualised the country's actions and suggested that it was still scarred from its 1954 Geneva experience. In an attempt to counter the Brezhnev Doctrine, he attempted to play on the Kremlin's self-interest in preventing a North Vietnamese victory that "would deprive an American president of any authority to have the sort of discussions with the General Secretary that it has been the principal objective of his Administration to bring about." Kissinger claimed to have meant the comment in a "spirit of understanding," but he was trying to turn the Brezhnev Doctrine against its author. When Brezhnev criticised the bombing of North Vietnam, he responded, "You were hinting at Czechoslovakia." Kissinger claimed to have meant the comment in a "spirit of understanding." Brezhnev was not going to back down. The general secretary continued by asking if the bombing would aid Nixon in winning reelection. However, he soon turned his attention to the Chinese, claiming that they were responsible for the Vietnamese offensive because "we have nothing to do with the planning of the war."

On April 24, Kissinger arrived at Camp David in the evening. That same day, press reports indicated that there had been another "catastrophic" onslaught in the Central Highlands by the North Vietnamese. According to Haldeman, Nixon was all primed to really whack Henry," but once Kissinger showed up, he backed off in typical Nixon fashion. Nixon's fly being unzipped during the meeting did not help his projection of presidential authority.) The following morning, Nixon joked about where Kissinger was when he was trying to get in touch with him, and Nixon's secretary RoseMary Woods responded, "Probably out with some babe." Kissinger laughed and said no, but "it wasn't through a lack of offers." He then regaled Nixon with an account of how the Soviets had offered him "a whole bunch of girls, all 25 years and younger," and that "the crudeness of these guys is not to be believed." Nixon admitted to having "mixed emotions" regarding Kissinger's emphasis on the summit during his discussions with Brezhnev. Nixon stated, "We're going to be sorely tempted to save the summit at almost any cost," but he was willing to take a bigger chance. Kissinger disarmed Nixon by agreeing with him, but she also made the case that the Russians were now attempting to be helpful by passing American peace proposals to Hanoi. Nixon put the question in domestic terms, stressing again his feeling that the United States could not lose in Vietnam, "that this is the great struggle between the left and the right, the great struggle between the peaceniks and the patriots." Telling Nixon a narrative from Dobrynin, he made Nixon feel good by saying that he, Kissinger, had been quite strict with Gromyko. It was precisely the kind of reputation Nixon desired with the Russians, as Dobrynin later told his colleagues on the Central Committee, "If you think Kissinger is tough, wait till you meet the President."

Nixon delivered another prime-time speech on Vietnam in response to the favourable press surrounding the Kissinger visit. Nixon declared that the process of Vietnamization "has proven itself sufficiently" to permit the removal of twenty thousand more American forces from Vietnam, bringing the total number of Americans out of the country since he took office to half a million. General Abrams' assessment, which Nixon used, said that the South Vietnamese were defending themselves bravely and effectively. The invasion force is suffering huge losses as a result of their actions, and three weeks ago, some people had expected that it would win easily. Nixon declared that although the US would resume open peace negotiations in Paris, he would not stop airstrikes on North Vietnam. Recalling his "historic journey for peace" to China, he gave the audience the assurance that, in light of "Dr. Kissinger's report," he anticipated travelling to Moscow in a comparable manner. But he also cautioned that 'if the United States violates the millions of people who have counted on us in Vietnam,' such a journey will not be conceivable for future presidents.

As Nixon was meeting with Kissinger and Haldeman at the White House after returning to Washington from a fundraiser in Texas, the Abrams cable arrived on Monday evening, May 1. Brooding over the

Abrams cable, Nixon finally concluded that if South Vietnam collapsed, the United States could impose a blockade and demand its prisoners back. Nixon told Haldeman, during the flight from Texas to Washington, that he suspected, because of Kissinger's commitment to the summit and to the possibility of a breakthrough in negotiations with the North Vietnamese, that "Kissinger was not playing it straight with him on Vietnam" and that his national security adviser was "wrong on public opinion ». Kissinger concurred that option would be the sole one. Kissinger attempted to offer some consolation by saying the jaded cliché "We'll have to tighten our belts," but Nixon "sort of laughed" at the remark. Nixon then somberly said, "But then we're defeated." Nixon realised that "we may have had it in Vietnam" and that this would mean the end of his political career. This was reflected in the "sort of laugh" that he expressed.

Nixon told Kissinger "not to give anything" before he went to Paris the following day, and he knew that the president was prepared to call off the meeting and issue an order for "hard strikes" if the North Vietnamese demonstrated a genuine desire to engage in negotiations. Nixon's message to Hanoi was summed up as "settle or else." However, the North Vietnamese did not see the need to give in given what was happening on the battlefield. Kissinger met with Lê Đức Thọ and Xuân ThÚy for three hours, during which time he only reiterated his previous statements. In exchange for the prisoners of war, Kissinger suggested a four-month cease-fire and an American pullout. Kissinger became agitated when the Vietnamese kept bringing up American domestic politics, and he snapped, "Our domestic discussions are of no concern of yours." Lê Đức Thọ pulled Kissinger aside as they were leaving the meeting to comment on how "good" the prospects for the North Vietnamese now looked. Kissinger subsequently told Dobrynin, "The man was as defiant as if he had won the war after all."[6]

Nixon saw that "there really isn't enough in it for the enemy to negotiate at this time," and he was not surprised that Kissinger had little success in negotiations with the North Vietnamese. Nixon noted in his diary that Kissinger's "weakness" was his obsession "with the idea that there should be a negotiated settlement." Nixon now felt that he needed to take strong military action against the North and to undertake a step that even Lyndon Johnson had hesitated to take: mining the harbour at Haiphong. In contrast to earlier bombing campaigns, the North's conventional military onslaught in the South was largely dependent on a daily supply of imported fuel for its tanks and armoured vehicles. As such, any disruption in that fuel supply could have major consequences. However, mining Haiphong meant that there might be direct interference with Soviet shipping, which Kissinger referred to as "crossing the Rubicon." This put the Moscow summit in peril and raised the question of whether the US should call off the meeting before the Soviets. Additionally, Nixon made it plain that he could not attend the summit, reach a deal with the Soviets, toast each other, and sip champagne while the North Vietnamese marched into Hue or Kontum, armed with Soviet tanks and equipment. John Connally and Haldeman both argued that the United States should take whatever military action it saw appropriate and let the Russians determine whether or not to call off the meeting rather than acting first. Connally's "animal-like decisiveness" won Nixon over when he told him, "You can live with a defeat in Vietnam, but you can do without the summit."

Kissinger argued both in favour of and against each course of action, but the idea of failing the Moscow summit still "horrified" him. His covert negotiations had advanced the SALT pact significantly, as the Russians demonstrated a readiness to make concessions on the ABM issue as well as the treaty's inclusion of submarine-launched ballistic missiles (SLBMs). Kissinger believed that the destiny of South Vietnam was not nearly as important as the possibility of reaching the first major arms control deal between the superpowers. He was "agonising about his image with the liberal community," hoping to avoid becoming what he often referred to as "the Walt Rostow of the Nixon Administration," and he was "uncomfortable" with the direction Nixon was heading, stating to sympathetic journalists that Vietnam "still had the capacity to distort the nation's diplomatic priorities." He also expressed his fear that renewed bombing "would trigger every goddamn peace group in this country."

Kissinger made the decision to comfort the president after observing the direction that Nixon was taking. Nixon expressed his complete agreement as he graphically spoke of his wish to "flush Vietnam down, flush it, and get out of it in any way possible and conduct a sensible foreign policy with the Russians and with the Chinese." Kissinger exclaimed, "Goddamnit, let's face it, if they had accepted our May 31st proposal last year, they would have taken over Vietnam within a year or two." Nixon replied, "See, if we can survive past the election, Henry, and then Vietnam goes down the tubes, it really doesn't make any difference." Nixon then returned to the initial motivator Kissinger agreed that it was "as cold as that," but Nixon quickly agreed, adding, "Don't be so careful that you don't knock out the oil for their tanks." Kissinger then shot back, saying, "The only point I disagree with is we can do all of this without killing too many civilians." Nixon, on the other hand, strongly agreed.

Kissinger adjusted once Nixon made his decision, but he still thought the Russians would call off the conference. He insisted that Nixon's speech be "calm and low key" and "extremely conciliatory to the Russians," implying that it should be in stark contrast to Nixon's theatrical statement on Cambodia. Once more, Nixon nodded and informed Kissinger that "the bombing is the only area where you and I are at odds right now." After Kissinger left the room, Nixon told Haldeman, "Henry's always saying he's going to get something out of the Russians," and he "really shouldn't be lunching with Dobrynin today." But Nixon did not stop him, and Kissinger met with his

Russian counterpart, explaining that Nixon had made the decision to go to the summit but not warning him about the mining. Kissinger justified his concern by appealing to Nixon's self-interest, noting, "I'm concerned about the civilians because I don't want the world to be mobilised against you as a butcher." Dobrynin's advice to his superiors at the Kremlin was to "try to refrain from making particularly major decisions on far reaching military measures" against North Vietnam until the summit.

Nixon urged Kissinger to give a press briefing the following day in an attempt to diffuse and placate the opposition. Marvin Kalb felt certain that "Henry didn't have his heart in it," but according to other reporters, Kissinger offered a "passionate defence" of the president's decision. Kissinger described the move as a "very painful and difficult decision," made "only because it was believed that no honourable alternative" existed, in a voice that was "choked with emotion." Kissinger stated that the summit conference was still on and expressed hope that the Soviets would respect the American choice, but he would not forecast their response. CBS stated that Kissinger's voice raised "in anger" when he accused North Vietnam of trying to humiliate the United States, despite the fact that they were still not allowed to use the audio of his briefing. After calming down, Kissinger spent the majority of the briefing assuring the Soviets of the advantages of working with the United States and pleading with them to "work out some principles of international conduct" that would enable the successful management of such problematic peripheral conflicts as Vietnam. Behind closed doors, Kissinger called Dobrynin to inform him that he had spoken with Willy Brandt's assistant, Egon Bahr, and received assurances regarding the ratification of the German treaties. "I wanted you to know that we have continued to do business as we promised," Kissinger continued, at least in regions outside of Southeast Asia.

The tension was short-lived. Kissinger asked Ambassador Dobrynin if he could set up some publicity, and the Russian agreed, when the Soviet foreign trade minister Nikolai Patolichev and Dobrynin arrived at the White House on Thursday, May 11, for a meeting with President Nixon. The end result was a lead story on NBC's evening newscast that featured a friendly gathering between Nixon, Kissinger, and the two Russians. A reporter then shouted at Patolichev to ask if the president's visit was still scheduled, to which he replied, "We never had any doubts about it," through his interpreter. Kissinger's assessment of the summit's likelihood drastically changed, and he now informed Nixon of several indicators that pointed away from a cancellation. He called Nixon early the following day, informing him that the Soviets' decision to cancel was "slightly better than 50–50," and that if they did so now, it would take them eighteen months to return for another summit. By late afternoon on that same day, Kissinger reported to Nixon that he had met with Dobrynin, who was "busily working away at the summit," and they were discussing various gifts to give each of the leaders. Nixon realised the political significance of this and told Kissinger, "If they cancel this they're gambling on somebody else winning the election." Kissinger now believed that there was a "99 percent" chance the conference would happen. "Hanoi must be beside itself," he continued.

Nixon and Kissinger knew that their conversations in Moscow would be compared to the China trip by the media, both in terms of tone and content. Making sure that the vast array of agreements being signed in Moscow—including those pertaining to trade, arms control, scientific collaboration, and cultural exchange—were seen as presidential initiatives was a top concern. Nixon ordered Kissinger to bring Dobrynin to Camp David a few days before the summit, telling him that it was crucial that the Russians not disclose the Kissinger-Dobrynin back channel in their statements. Kissinger reassured Nixon, saying, "We can demonstrate that of these agreements not one could have been done without your personal channel to

Brezhnev." Nixon bluntly told Dobrynin, "I do not rely on Rogers," expressing a preference for meetings with Brezhnev to be limited "to the smallest number possible." Nixon hoped that Secretary of State Rogers could be kept "busy" at the summit by the Soviet foreign minister Gromyko, allowing Nixon and Kissinger to conduct the serious negotiations. Nixon and Kissinger, confident that they would "piss" on either SALT or the "principles agreement" as they had with the Shanghai Communiqué, joked crassly about Rogers and the State Department away from Dobrynin. Nixon lost it when he learned that Rogers was scheduled to hold a press conference to discuss the summit. He told Haldeman that he would be conducting the briefing and that Rogers "doesn't know the first thing about what is going on."

Nixon was concerned about the domestic political response to whatever agreements he may bring home, in addition to the bureaucratic politics of the summit. He cautioned Kissinger that even if he could convince them of the overall strength of the American deterrent, the real issue with a SALT agreement would come from the right and that it would be "terribly difficult" for them to accept that we "put our arms around our enemies." It would also be difficult for them to accept the numerical inferiority inherent in a SALT agreement. Nixon never really cared about the exact specifications of the quantity of missiles, the size of the silos, or the locations of the radars. Kissinger called, and Nixon said, "As you and I both know, it doesn't make a hell of a lot of difference," referring to a conversation he had with Dobrynin regarding the maximum number of radars that may be permitted at an ABM site. Just so we can defend it." Nixon's concerns about averting "a massive right wing revolt on the SALT agreement" grew after his decisions in Vietnam, which his conservative supporters had enthusiastically backed. The president's commitment to advancing new weapons systems like the B-1 bomber and technological advancements like the multiple independent reentry vehicle (MIRV) for warheads, which were not covered by the agreement, would have to comfort the hawks in Congress.

But none of these particulars mattered as much to Nixon as the summit's pure spectacle, which his advance men had once again skillfully staged. The Soviets informed Nixon that the public would greet him in a more "subdued" manner due to Vietnam; yet, correspondents estimated that over 100,000 Muscovites turned out to see Nixon's motorcade, in contrast to Beijing's deserted streets. The network anchors made a special effort to discuss how "remarkable" it was that the meeting was taking place in light of the events in Vietnam. Many agreements were signed in time for each evening newscast, highlighting the "substance" of these sessions and drawing comparisons with the China summit. The first night's accords on health and the environment were duly reported by the media, which portrayed the agreement on space cooperation as a true "twenty-first century" accomplishment of the summit. Nixon attended the Bolshoi Ballet, laid a wreath at the Tomb of the Unknown Soldier, and addressed Soviet TV viewers directly. These ceremonial ceremonies received a lot of airtime on television. NBC's presenter John Chancellor described Kissinger as "the second most important American" at the summit, and this fact was mentioned in the backdrop of several of their stories. As the two superpowers were "learning to be equal partners in the preservation of peace," Kissinger utilised his briefings with the media to persuade them of the meetings' historic significance. Additionally, he painted the encounters as a real historical watershed, perhaps even as "the end of the Cold War," and as a "healthy and civilised" method for the two superpowers to interact with one another.

Even though the summit was mostly staged by Nixon's team, there were a few unanticipated dramatic moments. Nixon and Kissinger were essentially "kidnapped" by Brezhnev on the third day and taken at a high speed to his dacha outside of Moscow. There, Brezhnev, Alexei Kosygin, and Nikolai Podgorny—the triumvirate of the

Kremlin—harassed the Americans over Vietnam for over three hours. Nixon patiently endured the verbal abuse, occasionally cutting in with a sharp remark such as, "Who elected the president of North Vietnam?" When he was eventually given more time to speak, he passionately defended his course of action before concluding, "We will think matters over," and "Perhaps Kissinger will use his brain to come up with a new proposal." After saying, "He must certainly do that," Kosygin responded, and Brezhnev adjourned the meeting. The meeting's news helped to cast the media's coverage in a more sceptical and negative light. The U.S.-Soviet relationship's "thorn of Vietnam remains," according to reporters, who also stated that Vietnam was "clouding the summit" and causing the arms control and trade negotiations to break down.

Actually, Vietnam had not had a major impact on the SALT negotiations. Nixon gave Kissinger permission to push the Russians for concessions while accepting the previously agreed-upon missile count limitations. Nixon gave him this go-ahead as Kissinger described it as "a heroic position from a decidedly unheroic posture," as the president reclined in his Kremlin apartment, naked on a massage table. Though Nixon urged, "The hell with the political consequences," and Kissinger argued that Brezhnev needed SALT even more than Nixon did, it is hard to believe Nixon would have left Moscow without signing the first strategic weapons accord. Working against a Friday deadline, Kissinger and Gromyko engaged in an excruciatingly drawn-out negotiation that continued late into the night. As a result, a hurried compromise was reached on silo enlargement and the computation of Soviet SLBMs, both of which turned out to be confusing and advantageous to the Soviets and would later come back to haunt Kissinger during the SALT II negotiations. Still, the networks praised it as "the most important arms agreement ever," and Chancellor said that Richard Nixon had a "quite a day." It was evident how crucial Kissinger was to the president's success narrative amidst the widespread acclaim for his victory, which had overtly political implications. Informing the media about the accord, Kissinger was a key player. Kissinger "laboured with all the eloquence and brilliance at his command, along with a dash of sardonic humour, to minimise the vulnerabilities," according to John Osborne of The New Republic. The newscasts featured Kissinger's defence of the agreement, his assertion that "both sides won," and his characterization of SALT as in "the common interest of humanity," in addition to his thorough justification of why the agreement was balanced in spite of the Soviet Union's numerical advantage in ICBMs and SLBMs. He told reporters that the United States would not fall further behind the Soviet Union in the weapons race if ICBM manufacturing was stopped and submarine production was limited. He also indulged in his signature comedy. As he responded to a question, Kissinger deadpanned, "If I get arrested here for espionage, gentlemen, we will know who is to blame." Kissinger had never publicly discussed the Soviet Union's manufacturing of missiles.

The "Basic Principles" agreement, which defined the relationship between the superpowers, was the summit's final act and was signed after the SALT agreement. According to the declaration, the two nations "will proceed from the common determination that conducting their mutual relations on the basis of peaceful coexistence is the only option in the nuclear age." Walter Cronkite, the CBS anchor, now said that Nixon's trip had gone above and beyond expectations, and that while there had been no final agreement on trade or Vietnam, both agreements "paled into insignificance" in comparison to SALT and the Basic Principles accord. All of this, according to Cronkite, was "the personal accomplishment of President Nixon's diplomacy," and he and Kissinger had established a foundation of friendship and respect between the leaders of the Soviet Union. The spectacle of the summit and the pundits' treating it as "historic" were enhanced by Nixon's dramatic return to the United States, which included an evening helicopter landing on the Capitol steps to report to Congress and a live national audience. Nixon used strong language in his speech, urging Americans to "lead the world up out of the lowlands of constant war, and onto the high plateau of lasting peace" and to take advantage of this "unparalleled opportunity to build a new structure for peace." Henry Kissinger was seated next to Mrs. Nixon in the congressional gallery, grinning and giggling. After Moscow, the presidential party stopped briefly in Tehran, where the morning newspaper photograph of Kissinger in a nightclub was the subject of jokes among the newscasters. When asked about their discussion of "how you convert the SLBMs on a G-class submarine," Kissinger said that the national security adviser had a belly dancer perched on his lap in the photo.

In the summer of 1972, Kissinger was a regular on the nightly news, with his trips across the world reported and his remarks analysed for any hint that the peace negotiations with Vietnam were moving forward. As the president's "number one envoy" and a "man with one of the toughest jobs in the world," Kissinger's covert excursions were now a thing of the past, with reporters trailing him like the paparazzi of modern times. In August, Kissinger went to Paris for negotiations with the North Vietnamese before returning to Switzerland to celebrate his parents' 50th wedding anniversary with his kids and other family members. While present, CBS News hoped to obtain an evaluation on the peace negotiations. At the Republican National Convention, Henry Kissinger was a distinguished guest. Walter Cronkite said that floor reporter Dan Rather had secured an interview with a "celebrity," Henry Kissinger. Kissinger emphasised in this interview that "peace is much too important to be engaged in partisan politics" and that the government was making "a very serious effort" to negotiate an end to the war. He also said, very straight-faced, that the president "never talks to me about domestic politics," a claim made more for the image Kissinger wanted to present than for any real validity. Additionally, he starred in the Nixon-focused

Republican campaign film that emphasised both the visit to China and the meeting in Moscow. Initially, Kissinger acknowledged in his contribution that he had disagreed with Nixon, just like "most of [his] colleagues," but that he had watched and studied him and now believed that there was "a certain heroic quality about how he conducts his business" and that his influence on foreign policy would be "historic."

Though their disagreements over particular strategies and the timing of initiatives occasionally surfaced, Nixon and Kissinger shared the desire to terminate the conflict. Early in August, when they spoke about Vietnam, both of them expressed doubts about South Vietnam's long-term survival, but Nixon's major worry was that the Saigon regime needed to hold on until after the November election. Nixon stressed, "We also have to realise, Henry, that winning an election is terribly important, it is terribly important this year," keeping the domestic political ramifications front and centre. Kissinger concurred and said that "by January '74 no one will give a damn" if they could get a proper settlement by October in response to Nixon's query about whether the US could maintain a "viable foreign policy" if North Vietnam overran South Vietnam in a year or two. Nixon was more concerned about raising expectations among American voters each time Kissinger met with the North Vietnamese in Paris than he was about the negotiations, as Kissinger was more upbeat about the outcome—a lesson from the 1968 election. Nixon did not, however, prohibit Kissinger from holding more meetings in Paris.

Kissinger was right in his assessment of his opponents. In the summer of 1972, Hanoi's politburo altered its policies, perhaps as a result of a confluence of factors including the defeat of its military campaign, general war fatigue among the populace, and pressure from both the Soviet Union and China. Nixon's May 8 address contained recommendations that North Vietnam eventually agreed to, including the separation of the political and military facets of the negotiations. In exchange for the United States withdrawing completely from Vietnam, Hanoi would now consent to an established cease-fire, with North Vietnamese soldiers remaining in the South, and the release of American captives. The Communists and Saigon might resolve their differences "peacefully" through elections with ambiguous boundaries, and the Thiệu government could continue in office. Now, Hanoi demanded a settlement before November 7, the U.S. presidential election day.

But Saigon was not interested in a deal. President Thiệu thought the conflict was over when the ARVN soldiers were able to repel the attack. With the North Vietnamese forces still present in the South, the South Vietnamese were resistant to the idea of an all-out American withdrawal. The United States did not intend to leave behind any American military forces that may prevent a North Vietnamese attack, in contrast to its ongoing presence in South Korea. (The North Vietnamese demanded that the American POWs be released in exchange for their total evacuation.) The Vietnamese would face their devoted and resolute Northern brethren in combat, despite their superior financial and military resources. Like many of his fellow countrymen, Thiệu was frightened by the idea and resolved to oppose it, just as he had done in November 1968. "Thiệu's domestic imperatives imposed intransigence," as Kissinger acknowledged.

"They repeatedly, and almost plaintively, asked how quickly we wished to settle and there was none of their usual bravado about how U.S. and world opinion was stacked against them," Kissinger told Nixon after a meeting on September 15, sensing a shift in Hanoi's attitude. When Nixon learned that Kissinger had warned the North Vietnamese, "You and your friends have turned this election into a plebiscite on Vietnam," Kissinger was flattered. Additionally, the President will have support from a majority after November to carry on with the war. Nixon was less clear-cut. He cautioned Kissinger that according to his surveys, Americans preferred continuing to bomb Saigon and some even wanted "to see the United States prevail after all these years," not pressing the country to accept a coalition government with the Communists. Nixon was aware that the public's opinion was extremely "fragile" and subject to shift, and that pursuing the conflict might be detrimental to his newly formed alliances with China and Russia. Nixon was lured by the political advantages of a peace solution before the election and having the POWs "home by Christmas," despite his continued concern about a public showdown with Thiệu. This would mean applying additional pressure to Thiệu. Nixon urged Thiệu to "take every measure to avoid the development of an atmosphere which could lead to events similar to those we abhorred in 1963 and which I personally opposed so vehemently in 1968" in a letter he wrote on October 6, 1972, at Kissinger's request. Thiệu's fears were piqued by both references. If Thiệu refused to go to Paris for the peace negotiations in 1968, he believed Johnson was planning to topple him. The allusion to the Diem assassination in 1963, which was as menacing a warning as any American president could have issued, was even worse. It is difficult to understand why, but paradoxically, Ambassador Bunker told Kissinger that the letter "had a reassuring and steadying effect on Thiệu."

The encounter that took place two days later between Kissinger and Lê Đức Thọ turned out to be "the moment that moved me most deeply" in Kissinger's public service career. The U.S. plan, according to the Vietnamese ambassador, "represented an acceptance of our proposals," which included a cease-fire, the departure of American forces, the return of prisoners of war, and the separation of the military and political aspects of the solution. Furthermore, Hanoi acknowledged that Thiệu's government might continue to rule. Kissinger replied, "We've done it," shaking hands with his patient assistant Winston Lord after asking for a break. Others on his staff, most notably John Negroponte, reacted more subduedly, realising how hard it would be to persuade President Thiệu to accept the ongoing presence of North Vietnamese troops in the South. Kissinger, still full of victory, left Lord and Negroponte to finish Lê Đức Thọ's manuscript and went for a stroll in Paris. In a hurried telegram to Ambassador Bunker in Saigon, he informed President Thiệu that a cease-fire might be approaching and ordered his commanders to grab as much territory as possible. There has been some "definite progress" in the negotiations, he instructed Haldeman to report to the president, and he "can harbour some confidence that the outcome will be positive." Kissinger withheld the agreement's announcement until he could personally deliver the news to Nixon, sending similar ambiguous but upbeat communications throughout the course of the following few days.

On October 10, in a nationally televised paid political program, Senator George McGovern presented his own Vietnam strategy from back home in the United States. McGovern said he would stop bombing North Vietnam and stop providing any help to South Vietnam on Inauguration Day. He anticipated that the POWs would return if American soldiers were to be withdrawn in ninety days. Defense Secretary Laird denounced it as "unconditional surrender," but McGovern's speech made it plain that he continued to see political benefit in taking a staunch antiwar position and that the Nixon administration's support for the Thiệu regime represented a political weakness at home. Nixon was riding high on the back of a reasonably robust economy; the only things standing in the way of his potential landslide were the Watergate affair (The Washington Post published a front-page report on Republican spying against Democratic candidates on the same day as McGovern's address) and Vietnam.

After returning from Paris, Kissinger and Haig had dinner at the White House on October 12, 1972. Kissinger remarked to Nixon,

"Well, you got three out of three, Mr. President," without displaying any symptoms of jet lag. It will arrive soon. Surprised, Nixon said, "You got an agreement? Are you serious? Kissinger then went on to brief him on the specifics of the ceasefire and cease-fire he had negotiated with the North Vietnamese in Vietnam. Nixon became more enthusiastic—"cranked up," as Haldeman put it—as Kissinger proceeded slowly with his presentation, stressing that "this was a much better deal by far than we had expected." Nixon interrupted Kissinger to highlight all the difficulties and setbacks he had encountered in order to reach this point and considered the most effective strategies for persuading Thiệu to accept the treaty. Nixon finally made the decision to call in his valet, Manolo Sanchez, and request that he fetch the fine wine, a 1957 Lafite Rothschild, so that they might toast to the accomplishment. Nixon undoubtedly saw that Kissinger's agreement was not just another diplomatic coup but also the last straw that would have destroyed McGovern's chances of winning the presidency, since the North Vietnamese were now clearly willing to give Nixon far less than McGovern's Vietnam plan was demanding.

Kissinger and the North Vietnamese had worked out a strict timetable. The schedule stipulated that he would travel to Saigon to secure Thiệu's consent, then proceed to Hanoi for concluding discussions, with Nixon announcing the deal on October 26 and signing it in Paris on October 31, just seven days prior to the election. Kissinger would be at the centre of an amazing media spectacle if he could carry it off. In fact, a few of his less optimistic associates had suspicions that he was so enamoured with the idea that "the scenario was almost more important than the words" and that the haste to settle by Election Day might lead to carelessness on the finer points. Kissinger informed Haldeman that Thiệu would accept the arrangement despite all the evidence to the contrary, calling it "the best he's ever going to get and, unlike '68, when Thiệu screwed Johnson, he had Nixon as an alternative." Now that he has

McGovern as a backup plan, it would be far worse for him than anything Nixon could possibly do to him. Kissinger was given Nixon's word that he would make every effort to persuade Thiệu, but just before Kissinger departed, Nixon warned him once more that "we cannot have a collapse in South Vietnam prior to the election." Nixon was reassured by Kissinger that it would not occur. In the end, Nixon said to Kissinger, "Make the deal now if you can." Take the next best action if you are unable to. "It would be better for you politically to do the latter," Kissinger questioned. Henry, don't even consider the politics, Nixon retorted. To put it this way, both are advantageous.

Nixon was aware of the political ramifications, but he also thought he could manipulate the results to support his candidacy because he was leading the polls by a significant margin. The president was willing to wait until after the election if Thiệu refused to comply, but he believed that the solution that Kissinger had brokered was the best they could accomplish. Prior to the election, Kissinger desired the settlement. He thought this helped the U.S. position in negotiations since Hanoi was obviously eager to reach a quick settlement and appeared prepared to provide more compromises. Kissinger was aware that achieving this personal trifecta of diplomatic successes would bring him not just personal glory but also media attention, making him invaluable throughout Nixon's second term. It was obvious that Kissinger was becoming more concerned about his relationship with Nixon. He joked with his buddy Max Frankel, who requested an appointment, that "I am sometimes tempted to squeeze anybody in ahead of the President," and he told a reporter who wanted to do a piece on him "at home," "If I survive the next four weeks, you can do it." He called Nixon "my Leader" in several phone calls with understanding friends, while Nixon would sometimes joke with Kissinger about returning to the classroom, maybe at Pomona in California, and then say things like "poor Rostow, poor fellow's got to be in Texas and he's a brilliant fellow." We'll find you a decent college here, Henry.

Al Haig, Kissinger's deputy, sensed this unease. As a decorated combat veteran of the Vietnam War, Haig rose quickly through the ranks of the Nixon White House. Nixon valued Haig's physical bravery, loyalty, and straightforward demeanour. In contrast to Kissinger's disregard for these issues, Haig's organisational skills and military prowess ensured the efficient operation of the National Security Council. Haig was regarded by some in the White House as Kissinger's "alter ego," although this understated the competition between the two men for Nixon's attention. Kissinger's unease regarding his connection with Nixon was partly caused by Haig's intimate friendship with Nixon, which grew during Kissinger's frequent absences.

Haig informed Haldeman that Kissinger needed to have "complete support" in order to avoid feeling as though he needed to prove anything. But since Haig was also warning Nixon about Thiệu's resistance to settling, it's possible that Haig was playing a two-sided game given his own misgivings about the deal. Kissinger said subsequently that he was the least involved of Nixon's assistants in the election campaign and that the White House staff intended to "cut [him] down to size." I had declined to attend any fund-raising events because I believed that foreign policy was a matter for both parties to discuss. This wasn't the true problem. Kissinger's smug and contemptuous views of South Vietnamese people, whom he held in lower regard than his communist fellow countrymen, were the main source of the issue. Kissinger thought that Thiệu would have to submit. One of the main Vietnamese media published a fictitious naked photo of the national security adviser, Kissinger posing on a rug similar to how actor Burt Reynolds was photographed for the magazine Playgirl, the day after Kissinger arrived in Saigon. The caption read, "Kissinger has no more secrets." This indicated to Kissinger that he would not receive the same level of deference or respect in the Vietnamese city as he had become accustomed to.

According to his assistant John Negroponte, the encounter was "very tense and very unpleasant." During his intense confrontations with Thiệu's advisers, Kissinger faced challenges from Nha, his adopted nephew and cousin, regarding the Vietnamese text of the agreement. Nha specifically brought up a reference to only "three" nations in Indochina, which implied that Kissinger accepted the Communists' insistence that Vietnam was one country. Kissinger became so frustrated that he would frequently cancel appointments and arrive late, to the point where he would cry out, "I am the Special Envoy of the President of the United States." You understand that I can't be used as an errand boy. Thiệu flatly disapproved of Kissinger's compromise. Kissinger informed Nixon that it was difficult to overstate how strong Thiệu's stance was. His demands are almost insane. Nixon believed that Kissinger's desire to stick to the timetable he had set for Lê Đức Thọ and visit Hanoi in an attempt to get a final agreement would now appear to be "a complete surrender." The president issued another letter alerting Thiệu to the political ramifications of breaking with the United States and asked him to keep pressing Thiệu. Nixon believed that Kissinger might have some power with Thiệu because the US had already started Operation Enhance Plus, a large military aid program to Saigon intended to support the regime before a cease-fire. But like the first encounter, Kissinger's last one ended horribly. The National Council of Reconciliation was rejected by Thiệu, who also claimed that the US wanted to leave South Vietnam and refused to admit the existence of a North Vietnamese force in the country. "We have fought for four years, have mortgaged our whole foreign policy to the defence of one country," retorted Kissinger fiercely. It is quite painful to hear what you have said.

Kissinger was afraid that after his return to the United States, Hanoi would now make the arrangement public, indicating that it was willing to compromise and embarrassing the administration politically. In an attempt to break the news, Kissinger met with journalist Max Frankel of the New York Times for lunch and shared the main points of the deal as well as his own contribution to its acquisition. Kissinger was prepared to act when Radio Hanoi finally made the deal public on October 26th, the morning of the broadcast. "We believe that peace is at hand," he said during a nationally televised press conference. His audacious remarks dominated the evening news. Commentators around the nation were electrified by Kissinger's remarks, with some highlighting his pivotal role in the agreement's negotiations and others saying they ensured Nixon's landslide victory. Kissinger began a full-scale media attack following the press conference, conducting several interviews and briefings and creating, in the words of the Kalb brothers, "an extraordinary journalistic momentum behind the idea of 'peace is at hand.'" Kissinger's press appearance was hailed as "the best lucky break of the campaign" by Haldeman, who was generally concerned that the singer would overshadow Nixon. This was because Kissinger's remarks "takes the [Watergate] corruption stuff off the front pages, totally wipes out any other news." Later that night, Nixon joked to Kissinger over the phone, "I understand that all three network news shows were about Vietnam and I wonder why." With a laugh, Kissinger said that he had spoken with Colson, who thought that "we had wiped McGovern out now." Kissinger went on to say that he believed the president was receiving credit before the agreement was finalised. Nixon expressed his satisfaction to Kissinger, telling him that if he had made the statement himself, people would have assumed it was a political ploy.

Kissinger expressed his own views in a closing statement to the press that was not widely reported at the time. He concluded by expressing his hope that "we can restore both peace and unity to America very soon." He had previously stated that the United States would not be "stampeded" into an agreement, a reference to North Vietnam, nor "deflected from an agreement when its provisions are right," a reference to South Vietnam.155 Kissinger sincerely thought that the internal conflicts caused by the war would be healed by a negotiated settlement. It was also his means of projecting an air of nonpolitical expertise while delivering a forceful political message in favour of Nixon. However, his claims that "peace is at hand" quickly came under fire from detractors who wondered why the deal was still unattainable. Sen. McGovern claimed on Meet the Press a few days after Kissinger's press conference that Kissinger's remarks were purely political in nature. Later, at a campaign event on November 5, he accused Kissinger of lying, saying, "Peace is not at hand; it is not even in sight."

Kissinger was extremely confident in the days preceding the election, sure that the war would finish soon and that his own idea of a negotiated settlement would be realised. He subsequently described it as the "most disastrous conversation I ever had with any member of the press," and it was during this period that he had it. Kissinger would later strongly regret a number of remarks he made during two encounters with the Italian journalist Oriana Fallaci, among them being that his "movie star status" was largely due to his "lone action." That is very popular among Americans. Americans like the cowboy who rides ahead of the wagon train by himself on his horse. Aside from the query, "If I put a pistol to your head and asked you to choose between having dinner with Thiệu and having dinner with Lê Đức Thọ, whom would you choose?" one would wonder if he was flirting with the attractive Italian.—were intended to rile him. As enthralled journalists discussed the Vietnam negotiations and paired these with China and the Soviet Union, Kissinger explained that the cowboy was an amazing, romantic character that suited him precisely because being alone has always been part of my style, or if you like, my technique. This explanation leads one to conclude that Kissinger believed in his own magic. The idea that Kissinger was "Nixon's mental wet nurse" was put forth by Fallaci, but Kissinger shot it down, stating that Nixon was "a very strong man" with a "consuming interest" in foreign affairs and that "what I've done has been possible because he made it possible for me."158 These remarks, especially with regard to China, were insignificant in comparison to Kissinger's assertions that he took solo action. Strangely, they also mirrored the mindset of some of Nixon's most ardent detractors, particularly those on the right, whose thinly veiled anti-Semitism was evident in their exaggeration of Kissinger's participation. John Schmitz, the presidential candidate of George Wallace's American Party, told voters during his campaign that they "deserved President Kissinger for four more years" if they were "fooled by all this talk of peace" in Vietnam.

On election night, Nixon returned to the White House and discovered a handwritten note from Kissinger on his bed pillow. Thanking Nixon for his "unfailing human kindness and consideration" and for the "privilege of the last four years," it praised his "historic achievement—to take a divided nation, mired in war, losing its confidence, wracked by intellectuals without conviction, and give it a new purpose and overcome its hesitations." Nixon's resounding electoral triumph—49 states and 60.7% of the popular vote—was a noteworthy individual accomplishment in which Kissinger had been instrumental. Late on election night, Kissinger gave Nixon a call to offer his "warmest congratulations," during which Nixon labelled McGovern a "prick" for what he considered to be an impolite concession speech. Playing to Nixon's prejudices, Kissinger concurred, calling the senator from South Dakota "ungenerous, unworthy" and reminding him that despite the opposition of the media and "all the intellectuals," he still prevailed. Nixon, however, was still infuriated when the Fallaci interview was made public a week and a half after the election, despite Kissinger's words of support. Nixon was shocked when he spoke with Haldeman, especially after learning that Kissinger had claimed exclusive responsibility for the China effort. In order to remind Kissinger that decisions were documented and that, in Nixon's words, "[Henry] doesn't make the decisions, and when they are made, that he wavers the most," he even advised Haldeman to inform Kissinger about the White House taping system.

In the aftermath of the election, Kissinger worked to prepare for his trip to Paris while holding out hope that Haig would handle Saigon and win concessions from President Thiệu. Though the outcome of Haig's conversations with Thiệu was better than those of Kissinger, the problem of North Vietnamese forces in South Vietnam persisted. Haig expressed reluctance to escalate the matter to the point of an open break, stating, "To have done so would have hardened his position and confronted him with a test of manhood in front of his advisers that he could not have gone back from." Kissinger assisted Nixon in crafting a second, forceful letter to Thiệu, in which Nixon attempted to soften his hard line with Thiệu by stating, "It is my intention to take swift and severe retaliatory action." However, Thiệu's persistent defiance prompted Kissinger to lament, "That goddamn Thiệu—he's going through his stalling act." Kissinger informed Nixon that he could support a straightforward bilateral agreement with the North Vietnamese, despite his opinion being a "terrible" alternative. Kissinger feared that the North Vietnamese would harden their stance but told Nixon, "At this moment they are less of a problem than Thiệu." Both men realised that the newly elected Congress might vote to cut off assistance to Thiệu if he continued to resist the agreement. Nixon worried that antiwar critics would then be able to say, "Hell you could have done that all along."

Beginning on November 20, Kissinger's reopened talks in Paris were conducted under a media circus, with hundreds of journalists and television reporters following Kissinger around. In a classic example of overcompensation, Kissinger frequently emphasised during his arrival press conference that he was in close consultation with "our allied country, the Government of the Republic of Vietnam."

Kissinger continued, saying a "rapid" end to the war could occur if the North Vietnamese adopted the same positive outlook as they had in October. Kissinger's happy demeanour and strolls in the garden with Lê Đức Thọ were interpreted as indications that an agreement was imminent during the television coverage of the negotiations during the following weeks. Behind the scenes, Kissinger and the North Vietnamese made minimal progress toward implementing the sixty-nine reforms that Thiệu requested in the October accord. The North Vietnamese responded by withdrawing some of their earlier concessions, most notably now insisting that Thiệu release some thirty thousand political prisoners at the same time they released American POWs. He described Thiệu's changes as "so preposterous, they went so far beyond what we had indicated both publicly and privately, that it must have strengthened Hanoi's already strong temptation to dig in its heels and push us against our Congressional deadlines." Nixon reacted to Kissinger's report to the president by sending him a "tough-sounding instruction" that he could use with the North Vietnamese, reminding them that he was capable of taking "strong action," much as he had done prior to the Moscow meeting. Kissinger portrays an isolated Nixon as much more eager to use military force than Kissinger thought wise in his memoirs, where he is described as "ensconced at Camp David, surrounded only by his public relations experts,... deep in the bog of resentments that had produced the darkest and perhaps most malevolent frame of mind of his presidency." Actually, Nixon was truly unsure about this, and the following day he reversed his stance and instructed Kissinger to continue negotiations with the North Vietnamese.

The negotiations were briefly suspended, and Kissinger went back to Washington with Nixon to continue pressuring South Vietnam to sign the deal. Nixon also assured Thiệu that he would respond "with full force" if there were any infractions. Kissinger then left for Paris. When he returned on December 4, the media once again expressed excitement about the near prospect of a settlement and cease-fire in

Vietnam. Images of a grinning Kissinger and Lê Đức Thọ shaking hands opened all three networks' nightly newscasts, with speculation that some American prisoners of war would return home by Christmas. There was a stark difference between the talks' actual content and the favourable coverage. Kissinger's report to Nixon that evening opened with the dire words, "We are at a point where a break-off in the talks looks almost certain." Kissinger tried to extract more concessions from North Vietnam that would placate Saigon, but they withdrew more of their previous concessions, including a demand that the American civilian advisers leave the country, which would have made the American military assistance useless. With the "attractive vision they see of our having to choose between a complete split with Saigon or an unmanageable domestic situation," Kissinger now thought the North Vietnamese were playing for time. In his own opinion, the United States now faced two options: either sign the October agreement as it related to the Thiệu regime, or risk breaking off the talks, which could mean resuming military action against North Vietnam and the political fallout. Kissinger gave Nixon advice that would come as a shock, acknowledging that if the negotiations failed, "I will talk to you upon my return about my own responsibility and role." Kissinger also hinted at his resignation in this way. In order to "continue with your principled course until there was a sound and just peace, and you would underline this stance by combining firm military actions and a reasonable negotiating position," Kissinger advised the president to make another "stirring and convincing case" to the people on national television.

Innumerable cables were exchanged between Kissinger and Nixon over the course of the next two weeks. Kissinger expressed optimism following one negotiation session and pessimism following another, while Nixon counselled patience and negotiations in one cable and firmness and threats in another. There was hope and an anticipation of an early resolution in the television coverage. Later, Kissinger explained that his complicated connection with Nixon stemmed from his tense relationship with the president at the time, which was made worse by Kissinger's perception of Nixon's remote position. Kissinger claimed that Nixon was "cut off from the most experienced senior advisers, all of whom were with me, including Haig." Nixon, for his part, believed Kissinger was still emotionally "up and down," weakened in his negotiations by the sense that the North Vietnamese now had "that he has either to get a deal or lose face." Nixon rejected out of hand Kissinger's proposal that he rally the nation to support a renewed bombing campaign, telling Ehrlichman, "Henry doesn't seem to understand that." Kissinger would ruminate, writing out the issues on his yellow pad, all the while showered with the advice of his public relations geniuses. Or does he? This personal strain and rivalry between the two men, exacerbated by the Fallaci interview and their attempts to pin the other down, misses the extent to which they eventually came to the same conclusion: Hanoi was stalling a final settlement, biding its time until the rift with Thiệu became irreconcilable and Congress withhold funding. Nixon realised that he had to make a difficult decision regarding both Vietnams: he was convinced that Hanoi was stalling because it was "aware of our difficulties with Thiệu and the threats we have made." Kissinger informed Nixon, "Hanoi may well have concluded that we have been outmanoeuvred and dare not continue the war because of domestic and international expectations." At the same time that Kissinger came to this conclusion about Hanoi's position, President Thiệu delivered another defiant speech to his National Assembly, demanding the complete withdrawal of all North Vietnamese troops and referring to the National Council of Reconciliation as a "disguised coalition government."

Nixon, Haig, and Kissinger all together on the morning of December 14, 1972, to talk about their decisions. All those there "agreed that some military response was necessary," but they disagreed on the nature of that response, as Kissinger subsequently recounted. Nixon actually gave a lengthy speech to start, encouraging Kissinger not to give up and to keep in mind everything that had happened to them over the previous four years—"November 3, Cambodia, May 8th"—and not to question his recent decisions, such as the declaration that "peace is at hand" prior to the elections. Kissinger then gave an account of the Paris talks in a way that suggested there had been a sudden shift in the North Vietnamese position at the end of the third day of talks, which he had not reported earlier, and that after that point, they had started dragging things out. Kissinger apologised for his "up and down reports," saying that "they had us on a roller coaster." He suggested that the content of Washington's messages to Thiệu was leaked to the North Vietnamese by intelligence obtained from inside the Saigon government. Kissinger explained that he had continued to negotiate seriously until the very end, emphasising that on the last day he was there, "We had it down to two issues on the text, and one issue of substance." But in the end, Kissinger became convinced that "they're always going to keep it just out of reach," and without a deadline like Election Day, the North Vietnamese reverted to their "normal negotiating habit" of delay after delay. Nixon already suspected this, in part because the United States itself was listening in on Thiệu's internal conversations as well. Kissinger argued that Hanoi recognized this as well, and that the greater the possibility we would flush Thiệu down the drain. Kissinger cried, "They're shits, tawdry, miserable, filthy people." They enhance the Russians' image.

Kissinger did not confine his catholic scorn to the North Vietnamese alone. According to him, the United States was "caught between Hanoi and Saigon, both of them facing us down in a position of total impotence, in which Hanoi is just stringing us along, and Saigon is just ignoring us." This was, in one of Kissinger's favourite expressions, his "cold-blooded analysis," and he could see nothing changing. His "gamble" to get a settlement before the election was lost "80 percent because of Thiệu." At this point, Kissinger offered to disclose the impasse in the negotiations in a "low-key briefing" to the media. Because he "was the guy who said, 'Peace is at hand,'" he admitted that they would attack him. This self-sacrifice, carried out with a good measure of self-pity, caused Nixon to provide Kissinger with comfort and strategic advice on how to handle the press. Nixon even coined the statement that Hanoi wanted a treaty that provided "peace in North Vietnam and perpetual warfare in South Vietnam." Using one of Nixon's own idioms, Kissinger then suggested, "We start bombing the bejeezus out of them within 48 hours of having put the negotiating record out." After two weeks of bombing, Kissinger thought the United States should offer a separate deal to Hanoi, excluding Thiệu's government, that would trade the withdrawal of U.S. forces in return for the POWs and would be timed just as Congress came back into session. Nixon retorted that six months was not "in the cards" given the views of Congress, but they could bomb through Christmas and before Congress reconvenes. He continued, "If you are willing to go six months, they're going to crack." Nixon inquired about the use of B-52s after Haig mentioned that the weather in North Vietnam "is absolutely bad right now." As the meeting came to an end, Nixon worked himself up to the conviction that he had to order the bombing, that "we've got to play the big bullet." This time, though, he would not go on television "and make one of these asshole Vietnam speeches." Kissinger calculated that the chances were "75–25, because these guys are on their last legs." Kissinger quickly interjected to reassure Nixon that he was correct in this regard and that Kissinger had erred in suggesting it. "This is not the time." "It's painful for me... but if you don't do this, it will be like the EC-121," he continued, alluding to the absence of reprisals following North Korea's downing of an American spy plane in April 1969. Nixon repeatedly reminded him that "the professors are the enemy" and "the press is the enemy," so Kissinger adopted a phrase that would be guaranteed to catch his ire. "Mr. "If you don't do this, President, then you'll really be impotent," he emphasised.

Kissinger briefed the White House press corps about the impasse in the discussions on Saturday, December 16. Nixon had coached Kissinger extensively the day before, telling him to "make the President the tough guy all the way through" and informing Haldeman that Kissinger "must try to be effective rather than brilliant" after his departure. Equipped with Nixon's instructions, Kissinger attempted to hold Hanoi accountable for the impasse while simultaneously signalling to Saigon that a settlement was imminent. Kissinger made multiple references to the president throughout the briefing—fourteen times as opposed to three during the press conference in October. Kissinger's most frequently cited statement was, "The President decided we could not engage in a charade with the American people." He reiterated that the US would not be "stampeded into an agreement," adding that it would not be "charmed into an agreement until its conditions are right." Towards the end of the briefing, he did strike a conciliatory note, telling Hanoi, "We are prepared to continue in the spirit of the negotiations that were started in October." Ironically, Nixon's insistence on projecting himself as "the tough guy through" would eventually enable the narratives that Kissinger preferred diplomacy while Nixon wanted to bomb, tales that would earn Nixon a Nobel Peace Prize and bring him shame. At the time, Kissinger bemoaned the narrative that emerged from his briefing, which contrasted his report of a breakdown in the talks with his previous claim that "peace is at hand." This paradox was highlighted by NBC Nightly News on December 17, even before the bombing resumed. The show prominently included George McGovern's assertion that the administration purposefully misled the American people before the election. Additionally, it conducted a lengthy piece on Johnson City, Tennessee, Air Force Colonel Louis Taylor's death in Vietnam. The feature included an interview with Taylor's wife, who had supported Nixon but was now resentful that her husband had died as a result of peace being promised but not given. In his introduction, Garrick Utley listed the numerous deaths—mostly of Vietnamese descent, but also of Americans—that had occurred since Kissinger said that "peace is at hand."

Operation Linebacker II started on December 18 and lasted for twelve days, with a one-day break for Christmas. During that time, 739 B-52 missions dropped 15,237 tons of bombs on the areas of Haiphong and Hanoi. Five thousand more tons were dropped by fighter-bombers from the Air Force and Navy. Like a cowboy shooting his way out of the saloon, the American bombing attempt aimed to persuade the North Vietnamese to cease their delaying tactics and to reassure the South Vietnamese that the United States was not deserting them—a metaphor Kissinger would not have made today. The North Vietnamese shot down fifteen B-52s, nine fighters, a spy plane, and a rescue helicopter using nearly all of their SAM missiles. 1,312 casualties were reported in Hanoi by North Vietnam, and about 300 in the Haiphong region. Between 31 and 93 crew members were lost and seized during the operation for the United States. The "Christmas bombing" sparked a surge of vehement criticism of US actions from both inside and outside the country. Pope Paul VI referred to it as "the object of daily grief," the Swedish prime minister Olof Palme likened it to Nazi atrocities, and newspaper criticism across Europe was especially harsh. At home, Nixon's detractors blasted the bombing, with Senate Democratic Leader Mike Mansfield labelling it a "stone-age tactic" and Ohio Senator William Saxbe saying that the president "appears to have lost his senses." The operation was harshly criticised in the press and on television. The Washington Post headline read, "Terror Bombing in the Name of Peace." James Reston, a journalist for the New York Times, referred to it as "war by tantrum." Tom Wicker, a colleague, called it a "crime against humanity" while Anthony Lewis described it as "shame on earth" during the Christmas season. Some people personally addressed Kissinger. When Henry Kissinger, the "number one representative of the administration in foreign policy," declared that peace was on the horizon, Senator Stuart Symington claimed the White House had misled the American people. He asserted that other

Nixon administration officials had informed him that the government was not as near to peace as Kissinger had stated. According to Joseph Kraft, a pundit, Kissinger was "a good German" who gave legitimacy to "whatever monstrous policy" Nixon chose.

Kissinger had made direct appeals to the editors in an attempt to avert the Time award. Now, in his direct interactions with Nixon during the Christmas bombing, he attempted to reassure Nixon that his decision to bomb was the right one by trying to do something close to damage management. He informed Nixon that he had communicated to William Sullivan of the State Department, who accompanied him to the Paris negotiations, that "the President is caught between the two Vietnamese parties," and that their attempt to trap him was incorrect. Kissinger went on to flatter Nixon while highlighting his own point about how terrible both Vietnams are, particularly Thiệu. "I have no idea what [the president's] going to do, but my guess is he'll turn on both of them," Kissinger continued. Kissinger continuously berated Thiệu, calling him a "unmitigated selfish, psychopathic, son-of-a-bitch," and bemoaned that he had stopped the October deal, using language that was far stronger than what he used for the North Vietnamese. Kissinger also gave Nixon comfort, adding, "I have to have 200 letters or telegrams by now, all saying 'We are proud of what you're doing.'" Refrain from letting the Communists treat you badly. Additionally, he informed Nixon that "if we now get the agreement it makes it enforceable" through bombing. Nixon promptly consented, and Haig was dispatched to Thiệu just as the bombing began to inform him that the United States was getting ready to settle and to give him the assurance—supported by the B-52 bombing—that the United States would take action to stop any egregious North Vietnamese breach of the agreement.

But Kissinger was hurt by the heavy criticism he got for the bombing from friends and allies in the media, and he obviously tried to disassociate himself from the choice. In his memoirs, he describes how the White House staff attempted to hold him accountable for the discussions' failure and charged him with initially abusing his negotiating power. "Some of the journalists may have mistaken my genuine depression about the seeming collapse of the peace efforts for a moral disagreement," Kissinger concedes, though. The piece from Reston, which showed that Kissinger was "undoubtedly" against the bombing plan, was particularly noteworthy because it implied that Kissinger might step down and write a book about the Paris talks and their failure, which would likely humiliate Mr. Nixon. Nixon was so incensed by these articles that he gave his assistant Charles Colson instructions to phone Kissinger and instruct him to keep quiet. Nixon informed Colson, "I will not tolerate insubordination," and requested that the Secret Service maintain a log of Kissinger's phone calls. Kissinger subsequently acknowledged that his attempt to distance himself from Nixon on this matter "is one of the episodes in my public life in which I take no great pride," using the same language he used to express sorrow over the wiretaps on supportive media and his staff.

Kissinger was aware that the majority of congressional Democrats were committed to stopping funding for the war when he got ready to go for Paris in early January. While there were still liberal Republicans who opposed the administration's Vietnam policy and some conservative Democrats who sided with the administration, the Democrats controlled both the Senate and the House with comfortable majorities of 242–192 and 56–42. The House Democrats overwhelmingly decided on January 2 to stop funding as soon as plans were in place for the military to leave and the prisoners to return. A similar resolution was passed by the Democratic senators. Nixon angrily instructed Kissinger to forewarn Mike Mansfield that his attempts to serve funds would jeopardise his discussions and that the president would convey that message to the American people. Nixon and Kissinger were enraged by the congressional pressure, but they also used it to put further pressure on South Vietnam to make a settlement or risk losing financing and support.

Kissinger and Nixon were happy with the deal and resolved to get Thiệu to sign it. With letters from Nixon in hand, Haig was dispatched once more to Saigon. In them, Nixon informed Thiệu that he had "irrevocably decided" to sign the agreements on January 27 and that failure to do so would result in "an inevitable and immediate termination of U.S. economic and military assistance." Nixon promised Thiệu that the United States would "react strongly" in the event that the agreement was broken, using Operation Linebacker II as evidence of his integrity. Nixon instructed Kissinger to persuade John Stennis of Mississippi and Barry Goldwater, the former Republican presidential candidate, to convince Thiệu to accept the accord or risk having American funding withheld. Thiệu persisted in his resistance. Nixon and Kissinger both thought Thiệu was aware that rejecting the deal could result in his own downfall at the hands of other politicians. In Nixon's words, "They're down the tube" without the support of the US. Nixon remained concerned that Thiệu would turn down the offer and spoil the atmosphere for his second inauguration. "Do we have a plan... to cut our losses but God damned fast?" he questioned Kissinger. In response, Kissinger said, "Mr. President, the fact is that now we are doomed to settle," expressing his own sense of hopelessness toward Vietnam.

When asked about the over 150,000 North Vietnamese soldiers still in South Vietnam, Kissinger responded in detail. Kissinger attempted to paint the deal as something it was not during the NBC Nightly News coverage of his briefing by using the phrase "flat prohibition" numerous times, as though it had great significance. First, he asserted that the introduction of any new forces into South Vietnam was "flatly prohibited." He was making the argument that the number of North Vietnamese soldiers will eventually decline due to natural attrition. Then he said that there was a "flat prohibition" on any foreign forces operating in Laos and Cambodia, implying that no new North Vietnamese soldiers would be allowed to enter the South via these routes, which were part of the Ho Chi Minh Trail. It remained unclear how war-torn, weak Laos and Cambodia would carry out the prohibition. Third, he proposed that any force movement across the demilitarised zone was "flatly prohibited." Kissinger came to the conclusion that North Vietnam could not honour this agreement and continue to pose a danger to the South with its soldiers, even with the requirements for force reduction and demobilisation in place. "It is not inconceivable that the agreement won't be adhered to," he quickly added, but he hoped that it would be with the potential incentive of reconstruction funds and assistance from the Soviet Union and China. Following Kissinger, Lê Đức Thọ declared victory and refuted the existence of any North Vietnamese forces in the South in the subsequent NBC report. Lê Đức Thọ underlined that there was only one Vietnam, and the report suggested that he thought he had gained this issue in the pact.

In addition, Kissinger and Nixon emphasised the value of providing financial support to both North and South Vietnam, believing that this would give them some influence over North Vietnamese actions. At the conference on January 23, when the agreement was initiated, the North Vietnamese endeavour to obtain "ironclad assurances" of this economic aid surely confirmed to Kissinger that this may be a useful means of enforcing the deal. However, Kissinger's pessimism was also evident. After the press conference, John Ehrlichman asked Kissinger how long he believed the South Vietnamese could endure under the terms of the deal. He said, "I think that if they're lucky they can hold out for a year and a half."

Americans gave Kissinger a great deal of praise and admiration for pulling off his trifecta. He was ranked as the fourth most admired American by the Gallup Poll at the end of 1972, behind the late Harry Truman, Nixon, and Billy Graham. Nixon was enraged and irritated by Kissinger's actions during the final phases of the Vietnam

War, but he also recognized the tremendous contribution Kissinger made to his administration. Kissinger was "now the hottest property in the world," as he informed Haldeman following the details of the Vietnam accord to be known. Nixon could even make fun of Kissinger for being so aware of this. "Well, I hope your morale is all right," Nixon said to Kissinger as they were wrapping up the Vietnam negotiations. Nixon interrupted Kissinger in mid-sentence, saying, "You've been through a lot, haven't you?" "We've all been through a lot, but I think—" Kissinger retorted. Nixon interrupted, saying, "Well, that's my job." You know, you're only a hired hand. Nixon again cut Kissinger off as he tried to object, saying, "Now, Mr. President," adding, "I'm the guy that gets all the glory." Kissinger responded, "No President has taken such a beating, on the contrary, whenever you do something great, the press is looking for some way to take away the glory from you," and Nixon readily agreed. Kissinger did not want to accept the subtle irony in Nixon's comments.

There was an underlying competition as well as cooperation between the two guys. Nixon periodically fantasised about removing Kissinger, especially after reports like Reston's about the Christmas bombing. He was annoyed that Kissinger did not say more about his "courage" and other qualities in his January 24 press conference, complaining to Haldeman that, as Haldeman put it, "Henry should realise the way to show he and the P[resident] don't differ is for him to sell what the P[resident] did in his appearances, especially sell the hell out of the bombing." Henry was "the big gun," and Nixon wanted him to laud the president more. When Harry Reasoner, who only a year earlier complained about how dangerous a figure Kissinger was, now nominated him for the Nobel Peace Prize, Nixon informed Haldeman that Kissinger ought to answer Reasoner and support the president's role. But Nixon himself contributed to Kissinger's lyonization. In his first news conference after the Paris Peace Accords were signed, Nixon spoke of how Kissinger had "so brilliantly briefed the members of the press," and he speculated to Haldeman that part of Kissinger's problem was that "he's made all the big plays now and he's trying to look for ways to maintain the momentum, which is essentially impossible." As Time magazine had remarked, Kissinger was Nixon's brainchild, and an extension of his authority and political influence as president.

Chapter 4:Henry Kissinger Did It

On May 29, 1974, NBC Nightly News anchor John Chancellor declared, "HENRY KISSINGER DID IT." Along the Golan Heights border, Secretary of State Henry Kissinger had successfully negotiated a disengagement deal between the Syrians and Israelis. This accord was a remarkable testament to Kissinger's month-long "shuttle diplomacy," a term invented to characterise his constant trips between Damascus and Tel Aviv, as well as other Arab capitals, in quest of a peace agreement. It followed one between Egypt and Israel in January. Commentators were all praise for Kissinger's accomplishment. It prevented Israel from carrying out a military "blitz attack" against Syria that was scheduled in the days prior to the deal, as reported by NBC's David Burrington from the Golan Heights. It was also a major step toward a final Middle East peace and the lifting of future oil embargoes. As a result of Kissinger's work, hundreds of soldiers are still alive today on both sides of the border, according to Burrington. Declaring that this was "one of the most remarkable diplomatic efforts ever made," Chancellor ended the presentation by presenting Golda Meir, the Israeli prime minister, telling Kissinger that this was his day and his personal accomplishment. Kissinger was undoubtedly "the man of the hour," as he was dubbed by every network.

Kissinger had experienced the "trifecta" success of the first Nixon administration, but his current levels of notoriety and stardom were unheard of. Congressman Jonathan Bingham went so far as to suggest amending the constitution to permit the foreign-born Kissinger to seek the presidency. How had this come to pass? In what sense was Kissinger now the "president for foreign policy"? The most straightforward explanation was the catastrophic effect the Watergate affair had on Nixon's standing and his growing preoccupation with protecting himself from impeachment. But this story was about more than just Watergate and the shifts in US foreign policy that came with Kissinger's rise to power.

THE IMPACT OF WATERGATE

Kissinger had spent enough time in the Nixon White House to be familiar with the milieu of secrecy and even paranoia. He was well aware that one of the main goals of foreign policy was to ensure domestic political successes, even though he stated that "in the Nixon White House there was an almost total separation between the domestic and the foreign policy sides." The notion that leaks compromised the Nixon team's foreign policy presentation was the primary source of fixation, at least partially. Kissinger called Nixon shortly after he had his conversation with Garment, telling him that the most crucial item was "to protect the presidency and your authority." He advised Nixon to try to contain the controversy and cling on to Haldeman and Ehrlichman, "if humanly possible," even though he later referred to them as "men with a Gestapo mentality." Kissinger instantly replied, "That is out of the question," and "I don't think the President has the right to sacrifice himself for an individual," when an inebriated Nixon bemoaned having to fire Haldeman and Ehrlichman and said that instead he considered "throwing myself on the sword and letting Agnew take it." Kissinger was now assuming the stronger position in their chats, reflecting the gradual shift of power between them. Kissinger continued to tell Nixon that he had "saved the country," but he did it in a past tense and often cited history's eventual vindication of Nixon. Nixon responded by telling Kissinger not to give up on him again and time again, only to have his national security adviser firmly tell him that he was not. After Nixon called Haldeman on April 30, the evening before his national speech announcing Haldeman and Ehrlichman exits, he said, "Kissinger's reaction is typical; he's waiting to see how it comes out." When Kissinger called again the following day, he assured Nixon that although the press would "scream for a few more days" over his "unbelievably painful" and "tragic" decision to fire his two close associates, Watergate would eventually disappear "if there aren't any more major things coming out." Nixon abruptly halted the interview by laughing awkwardly and stating, "Oh there may be but what the hell."

After five individuals were detained in the DNC offices in June 1972, the Watergate affair gradually came to light. In the famous words of Press Secretary Ron Ziegler, the Nixon White House first wrote the story off as a "third-rate burglary attempt." However, The Washington Post dug deeper throughout the 1972 campaign, exposing the scope of the political sabotage and the links between the Committee to Reelect the President (CREEP) and the Watergate burglars. Nixon's landslide remained intact despite the coverage, leading many to believe that Watergate had likewise been buried. On January 30, 1973, the initial convictions, however, gave Judge John Sirica the authority to issue lengthy prison sentences and contributed to the case's public exposure. Early in April, Nixon's White House attorney, John Dean, started assisting the prosecution. Nixon was ultimately obliged to fire Haldeman and Ehrlichman after prosecutors and the FBI followed the money that had funded the Watergate Five to the White House. It also resulted in the disclosure of the "plumbers'" operations and the previous break-in at Daniel Ellsberg's psychiatrist's office. Nixon's general approval rating dropped from 67 percent in January following the Vietnam peace accord to just 45 percent in early May, and the noose around the president was starting to tighten.

Sadly for Nixon, Kissinger's active involvement in foreign affairs only served to confirm the belief that he was the true strategist behind Nixon's diplomacy. Kissinger's trips also prevented him from visiting Washington during the height of the media's fixation on Watergate. Kissinger went to Moscow a few days after Haldeman and Ehrlichman were fired in order to get ready for the Washington summit with the Russians. Kissinger was treated like a head of state by Brezhnev, who even invited him to the politburo's hunting park, Zavidovo. The Americans were wary, but the Soviets were determined to reach a deal on preventing nuclear war between the superpowers. In order to avoid seeming to Beijing as an alliance against the Chinese or to the European allies as a U.S.-Soviet condominium, Kissinger needed to sufficiently soften the terminology. In order to pull this off, Kissinger had quietly recruited Sir Thomas Brimelow, one of the best diplomats working for the British Foreign Office, to prepare the agreement while keeping Rogers and the State Department in the dark. Kissinger was able to successfully neutralise the language in Brimelow's draft and create a "marginally useful text" that Nixon and Brezhnev signed during their summit. Even so, despite Brimelow's influence in the agreement's formulation, the entire symbolism of a U.S.-Soviet accord infuriated the allies, including the British. Despite Kissinger's best efforts to persuade them that there was nothing new to be concerned about, the Chinese likewise maintained their suspicions. Kissinger was more concerned when, while on their wild boar hunt, Brezhnev managed to corner him and went on the attack against the Chinese, labelling them "barbarians" and urging the American, "We have to prevent the Chinese from having a nuclear program at all costs." This sounded suspiciously to Kissinger like the setup for an assault on China as a preventive measure.

But Vietnam continued to consume him. By mid-May, he was returning to Paris to resume negotiations with Lê Đức Thọ, even as the news of his permission to wiretaps gained widespread attention. Kissinger had expressed reservations in private but tried to project a public image of confidence ever since he signed the accords in January. In February, he told Barbara Walters of NBC that despite the fact that the fighting had continued a little longer than he had anticipated, he was not concerned that the cease-fire would fail. He responded with a firm "No" when she explicitly questioned if a return of American engagement was possible. He whispered at a

WSAG meeting that the government "should be one of extreme vigilance" on the ongoing infiltration of communists. He advised Nixon to "plan now for a 2-3 day series of intensive U.S. air strikes against the trail area of Southern Laos" two weeks later. However, Kissinger realised that Nixon was becoming less inclined to combine his domestic issues with any military action in Vietnam as Watergate started to consume him. "If we didn't have this goddamn domestic situation, a week of bombing would put them... this Agreement in force," he said to Nixon on April 23. Kissinger told the president quite plainly on May 2, following Nixon's national speech on Watergate, "We can't threaten them now." In public, Kissinger continued to urge patience, stating, "We are not pessimistic," on the likelihood that the Paris agreements will hold up.

Kissinger managed to dodge the commotion in Washington caused by Senator Sam Ervin's hearings by setting up a meeting with Lê Đức Thọ, with whom he conducted negotiations in Paris for over a month. President Thiệu requested that the North Vietnamese accept specific modifications to the formula that Kissinger negotiated, but the South Vietnamese were once again unable to sign another deal. Kissinger later said that the South Vietnamese were "in a mortal struggle for survival," and that "Saigon's concerns were better funded than its presentation of them." He was, however, more irate with Saigon at the moment, informing Nixon that Thiệu and his administration were in a "suicidal mood." "We are faced with a possibility of a Congressional Amendment to cut off all aid to Indochina," Kissinger said to the ambassador from South Vietnam, adding that a successful arrangement would help to delay action. Kissinger chastised Ambassador Phuong, saying, "I grant that our domestic problems are none of your doing, but you should appreciate our present position." After a lot of pressure, Saigon ``folded" and approved the joint communiqué that Lê Đức Thọ and Kissinger had written. During a news conference, Kissinger expressed his belief that all parties now realised that "nobody can have his way by force."

Kissinger's optimism that the deal would be successful this time was emphasised by the media and television coverage. The following day, however, he told the South Vietnamese, "This is the last time I am going to get involved in negotiations on Vietnam," adding dramatically, "I am washing my hands of this." He was certain that Hanoi was planning another invasion. Kissinger thought he had been freed from the "distraction" of Vietnam at last and was now ready to tackle the bigger challenges of great power diplomacy.

The wiretap story had mostly vanished by the time Kissinger arrived from Paris. After his return in June, Kissinger spoke with Nixon about his appearance in Congress where he defended his position against cutting off financing for military operations in Cambodia and discussed the joint communiqué with Hanoi. Despite the administration losing the vote, Kissinger told Nixon with pride that he received a standing ovation after his speech and that more than 150 congressmen wanted to have their photos taken with him. Nixon's reaction, "Great, that's the stuff," looked to be choked out of jealousy, showing his hopeless belief that this praise for Kissinger's work boded well for his presidency.

Nixon was temporarily relieved of the Watergate scandal during Leonid Brezhnev's visit to the United States in June 1973. During the summit, Kissinger took on a major public role, briefing the media about the expectations and attempting to present its accomplishments in the best possible light. As the two leaders decided to try to reach a SALT II agreement by the end of 1974, essentially reducing their nuclear arsenals, Kissinger told reporters that while defining nuclear weapon parity would be a difficult task, the United States would aim for "strategic parity." Kissinger could not help overstating the summit's importance given its cheerful environment and the apparent personal bond between Brezhnev and Nixon. In a muddled metaphor, he described this as "the beginning of a new period of international relations" and "a landmark on the road to the structure of peace" to reporters. Kissinger declared that this may result in "the fear of war itself" being lifted from all nations. Reporters saw "a sort of formalisation of the end of the Cold War," and he did not dissuade them.

While most Americans were relieved to see hostilities with the Soviet Union ease, they were considerably more captivated by the Watergate hearings in the summer of 1973. Approximately 80% of all households viewed a portion of these shows. Nixon's popular image suffered greatly as a result, as seen by the resounding congressional vote to terminate US bombing in Cambodia by August 15. Although Kissinger publicly expressed his opposition to the deadline, the White House declared that Kissinger's "next assignment" would be to work on a cease-fire deal in Cambodia prior to the deadline's implementation. In private, Kissinger thought, "There is just not much more we can do in Indochina." When Defense Secretary James Schlesinger confided in him, "Congress has to take the blame for the impending collapse of Cambodia," he unhappily agreed. At a July 6 news conference, Kissinger expressed his hope that China would exercise its "influence in the direction of restraint" and announced plans to visit Beijing in an attempt to secure a cease-fire prior to the implementation of the bombing halt. By now, North Vietnam had declared its support for Prince Sihanouk's comeback to power, and he had joined forces with the communist Khmer Rouge. On the other hand, the Chinese sent a message endorsing Sihanouk's insistence that the US withdraw its military presence and put Kissinger's visit on hold. Kissinger reacted instantly, taking this as a warning sign. He explained to a small group of advisers that the Chinese decision "to cancel a Kissinger trip was a major international event" because "he and the President were the key men who embodied American support for China for the right reasons." He had a suspicion that their policy had been altered due to Watergate and their belief that America was weak. A few days later, Kissinger's travel was simply suggested to be postponed by ten days in a second communication from the Chinese. Kissinger's overreaction demonstrated that his ego and emotions might override his "cold-blooded" realism. He personalised triangle diplomacy and China's strategy toward the United States far more than the Chinese had.

Kissinger was trying to talk Nixon into giving him the position of secretary of state even as he was considering the reasons underlying China's policies. Now serving as Nixon's chief of staff, Alexander Haig was vigorously pressuring Nixon to select Kissinger despite his deep desire to keep Nixon from granting Kissinger the increased autonomy and status that the position would bring. On July 13, CBS's Dan Rather announced that his sources verified Nixon's decision to name Kissinger as secretary of state, amidst a discussion on the president's treatment for viral pneumonia at Bethesda Naval Hospital. Fueling the flames was Secretary of State Rogers' refusal to respond to queries about these rumours when they were directed at him when he was in Japan for an economic summit. Although Kissinger maintained that the State Department was behind Rather's leak in an attempt to undermine his nomination, it is more likely that Nixon was forced into this decision by the leak. The president, already beleaguered by the disclosure of Alexander Butterfield's White House taping system and the news that Vice President Spiro Agnew was being investigated for his financial dealings as governor of Maryland, was further burdened by the implied threat that the well-liked Kissinger would quit if Nixon appointed anyone else. In an effort to maintain pressure, Kissinger told Nixon about a speech he had given praising the administration's foreign policies in order to highlight his significance. Kissinger boastfully informed Nixon, "And it was a tremendous ovation, and I had to fight my way out of there." He said, "It just shows that basically you have a lot of strength in the country," maybe recalling who he was speaking to. Nixon's clumsy response once more revealed his inner turmoil: "Yeah, ha, ha, right, right." Nixon felt compelled to appoint

Kissinger in lieu of Rogers. "Dr. Kissinger's qualifications for this post, I think, are well known by all of you ladies and gentlemen, as well as those looking to [sic] us and listening to us on television and radio," Nixon said to reporters on August 22, during his first news conference in five months, after announcing Rogers' resignation and lavishly praising him. Nixon reluctantly and grudgingly acknowledged that Henry Kissinger—his own Frankenstein monster—was now indispensable to keeping his administration intact.

THE FORTY-FOURTH SECRETARY OF STATE

The day following Nixon's statement, Kissinger conducted a press conference that was featured as the main story on all three network newscasts. He emphasised that he would prioritise foreign policy issues that had broad support and that his nomination marked the beginning of a "new era" in Congress and the president's collaboration on international affairs. He thought that this would "minimise" the impact of Watergate on international policy. Kissinger's response to the last query, which inquired if he would rather be called Mr. Secretary or Dr. Secretary, was shown on all three networks. "I don't adhere to protocol," a cheerful Kissinger stated. He went on, "If you just call me Excellency, it will be okay," to which the news anchors grinned and the press corps erupted in laughter. Kissinger subsequently claimed that he felt "oddly relieved," just as Churchill did when he was appointed prime minister following Dunkirk. He felt that now "one's convictions would stand or fall on their merits, without being strained through the uncertainties of clashing personal ambitions," alluding subtly to the internal drama of his battle with Rogers. Under the president's consent alone, he had unheard-of power as secretary of state and could carry out his own plans and ideas for US foreign policy. Actually, a beleaguered and distracted Nixon just nodded along. Kissinger realised that this was made feasible by Watergate. "After the Watergate revelation, I was the glue that held it together in 1973—and I'm not being boastful," Kissinger subsequently stated.

At the time, Kissinger was mainly unaware of these issues. Kissinger informed Nixon a few days after the coup started, when General Augusto Pinochet appeared to be gaining control, but the media were "bleeding because a pro-communist government was overthrown." Nixon joined him in bemoaning the fact that they now had to hide their role, whereas under Eisenhower they would have been looked upon as heroes. "Our hand doesn't show on this one," said Nixon, and "we helped them, creating the conditions as great as possible," said Kissinger. Kissinger made it clear later in the month that "we should not support moves against them by seeming to disassociate ourselves from the Chileans and on the other hand should not be in a position of defending what they are doing in Santiago" with reference to the Pinochet administration. This was after he had been confirmed as secretary. Kissinger's formal demeanour concealed his deep support for the new administration. Despite rumors of summary murders and torture, Kissinger was far more interested in ensuring that the new regime was aware of America's "good will" than in bringing up the subject of human rights. "That demonstrates the total naiveté of the new government," Kissinger sarcastically said when informed that the dictatorship was granting the press access. They are misguided if they believe the press is at anyway interested in the truth. Their only interest will be in horror research. Kissinger persisted in stating that "this government is better for us than Allende was," despite taking discreet action to secure the release of certain of the junta's detainees, notably the Communist leader Luis Corvalán. "Almost overnight, Washington reopened the spigot of bilateral and multilateral economic assistance to Santiago," as one policy critic put it. It's possible that Kissinger's hasty desire to assist Pinochet's dictatorship in solidifying its grip speaks more highly of his character than his prior efforts to keep Allende from becoming president. Kissinger was wholly unaware of how much the Chilean coup was "a watershed event" that helped "bring liberal human rights concerns... into mainstream public consciousness." However, Kissinger believed that in order for US foreign policy to fend off Soviet advances, it had to be pragmatic and even brutal in its willingness to form alliances with dubious regimes in the wake of the Vietnam War.

Regarding Chile, Kissinger pursued a course of action that was identical to that prescribed by Nixon. In the Middle East, on the other hand, a different kind of Kissinger policy began to take shape. American intelligence agencies were completely unprepared for the October 1973 "Yom Kippur" or "Ramadan" War, since they had not anticipated the unexpected attack on Israel by Arab armies under the leadership of Egypt and Syria. A week prior to the war, Kissinger had visited with Arab diplomats and left with the same impression. He was further persuaded that he would have time for any peace initiative after the Israeli elections by the assurances he received from Israeli officials. Recalling his remarks from the Indo-Pakistani war, Kissinger called Soviet ambassador Dobrynin as soon as Assistant Secretary of State Joe Sisco woke him up early on Saturday morning, October 6, alerting him to an approaching attack. At the start of the crisis, Kissinger had two main tasks in mind. The first was to maintain détente with the Soviet Union in an effort to minimise the effects of the war and hasten its conclusion. On the other hand, Kissinger believed that the second objective was to utilise the conflict as a springboard for a regional peace deal that would lessen Soviet dominance. Kissinger had opposed the Rogers Plan during Nixon's first term, claiming that such initiatives were too soon and unlikely to secure Israeli support. When he gave a background briefing in June 1970, he stirred much controversy by saying that the US wanted to "expel" the USSR from its position in the area. Kissinger, now in command of the process, was determined to thread the diplomatic needle and resolve the crisis in a way that diminished Soviet power without jeopardising détente.

In addition to showing personal confidence in his ability to handle the situation, Kissinger attempted to resolve the Middle East crisis on his own terms and refused to allow Nixon to exploit it for his own domestic political gain. Kissinger kept Chief of Staff Al Haig fully aware of his activities, but in an attempt to highlight his involvement in the issue, he instructed Haig to dissuade Nixon from wanting to return to Washington after his vacation in Key Biscayne. Haig said that Nixon was afraid of being perceived as "sitting in the sun" while a war was being fought, and that he would soon confront "a situation with Agnew." This was a tactful way of telling Kissinger that the vice president would be leaving soon. Nixon's worries were met with frank dismissal by Kissinger, who instructed Haig to rein down the president's "Walter Mitty tendencies." Kissinger clarified that the administration needed to avoid coming across as "hysterical" in its response because the majority of Americans would view the fight as a "local war." Kissinger pointed out that "this thing" might end in a day or two. The night after Vice President Agnew resigned, Kissinger even took a call from British Prime Minister Edward Heath, demonstrating the extent of his influence at that point.

Henry Kissinger was asked questions regarding the resupply of military material twice in the early hours of October 9 by the Israeli envoy, Simcha Dinitz, who had woken him up the first time. Dinitz relayed the devastating news to the secretary of state that Israel had lost 500 tanks and 49 planes in the first few days of the conflict when they met later that morning in Kissinger's office. After all, the Egyptian and Syrian armies exploited the element of surprise to effectively cross the Suez Canal and advance into the Golan Heights, causing significant casualties among the Israelis. Specifically, the Egyptian forces had inflicted significant damage because they were armed with mobile anti-tank guns. 500 tanks! Kissinger exclaimed, shocked. What number do you have? "So that's why the Egyptians are so cocky," Kissinger said in response to the Israeli military attaché's response of "1800." Reminding Dinitz of his own confidence that the Israelis would be victorious by now, Kissinger said to the ambassador, very subtly, "Obviously something went wrong." Dinitz informed Kissinger that Prime Minister Meir intended to covertly travel to Washington to make Israel's case to Nixon; Kissinger promptly dissuaded this notion. Kissinger realised at this point that his plan was doomed and that a "blowup" with the Soviet Union or the Arabs was far more possible. The prospect of Israeli nuclear weaponry in retaliation to an Israeli defeat at the hands of Soviet-backed adversaries was too much for the United States to bear. Kissinger was also aware of the Israelis' fear that "all the Arabs would jump in" if word got out about their defeats. However, taking decisive action to equip Israel by the US put détente at jeopardy and increased the likelihood of conflict with the USSR. Additionally, it might enrage the Arab nations and lead to the deployment of the "oil weapon." Domestically, Congress and the people overwhelmingly supported Israel, and Nixon's political standing may be severely weakened if Israel's dire circumstances were ignored. It must have looked to Kissinger the height of foolishness to declare the prospect of a foreign policy victory that he had stated the previous evening.

Kissinger's two aims were not entirely shared by other administration members. James Schlesinger, the secretary of defence, was significantly more dubious of Soviet intentions and questioned the wisdom of détente before war broke out. Kissinger was already at conflict with Schlesinger because of his resolve to alter American defence planning. In addition, he was angry by Kissinger's dominance over the WSAG crisis talks and his exclusion of other cabinet secretaries from the decision-making process. Schlesinger responded, "Okay, you are just watching the collapse of U.S. foreign policy," to a report from Thomas Moorer, the chairman of the Joint Chiefs, that the Soviet Union was preparing to launch "a massive airlift into the Middle East" at the same moment that Kissinger was assuring Dinitz of American support.

Kissinger's outward confidence obscured his deepening misgivings about Soviet actions. Shortly after the conclusion of the news conference, he informed the Israelis that he had received intelligence suggesting the Soviets had brought three airborne divisions into action, maybe in reaction to Israeli bombing operations on Damascus. Reports that the Soviet Union was pressuring other Arab nations, such as Jordan, to join the conflict also worried him. Dinitz arrived late that evening to complain that Israel's military offensive was being hampered by the slow pace of American deliveries. Kissinger called this a "disgrace" and pointed the finger at Schlesinger and the Defense Department, despite Schlesinger's explanation that the official policy was to maintain a "low profile" regarding American assistance and that American charter companies were not eager for business. Then Kissinger reassured Dinitz that, despite the lack of documentation, he had tried to expedite matters by calling Haig and Schlesinger every night. Insisting to Schlesinger that the "one thing we cannot have now given our relations with the Soviets is American planes flying in there," Kissinger now pressed for action, telling Haig, "I do not believe for one minute that they can't get charters if they tell these charter companies that the next time they need a rate change they won't get it." Kissinger still did not want American planes bringing the supplies directly to Israel. Schlesinger advised Haig to approach Nixon and request direct American action, telling him that Kissinger's plan would not succeed and that "anything else is acceptable." Nixon appeared energised by the necessity for a presidential decision, even though he was distracted with Watergate. He agreed with Schlesinger and told Kissinger to "do it now."

Kissinger had too brilliant a strategy when it came to helping Israel. By the end of the WSAG conference, Kissinger was calling Dinitz to inform him that the C-5As, some C-141 transports, and fourteen Phantom jets would be delivered, despite the fact that he was still expressing doubts. Kissinger rapidly adjusted and attempted to take advantage of the new circumstances, which went against his initial wishes. He now pressed Dinitz to temper Senator Henry Jackson's remarks by using his power. A congressional probe into the administration's handling of this situation was being threatened by the senator from Washington State. Reluctant to be undermined by any suggestion that the Nixon administration, or he personally, had "screwed up" on the Middle East, Kissinger told Dinitz, "Our whole foreign policy position depends on our not being represented as having screwed up a crisis, and with all affection for Israel, if it turns out that we are going to be under attack for mismanagement in a crisis, we will have to turn on you." Kissinger's elevated public image depended on continued success and the perception of highly skilled diplomacy, and he was told by Jackson that Israel has "never had a better friend than Dr. Kissinger." It was the pinnacle of the foreign policy personalization that Kissinger had come to advocate.

Following the meeting, Kissinger gave Nixon a call to inform him that the "Arabs are floating on air," that they understood Nixon to be "a great man" who talked to them with tremendous "sincerity," and that they would follow through on his promises to bring about peace in the Middle East. Kissinger's efforts to court Nixon were essential in reducing the tension that had developed between the two men as a result of Kissinger receiving the Nobel Peace Prize instead of Nixon—a move that Nixon found extremely offensive. After that, Kissinger informed Nixon that he had used the Vietnam negotiations to remind the Arab foreign ministers of the pressure Nixon had applied on Thiệu once the North Vietnamese had made a reasonable offer. Nixon enjoyed being reminded of that victory, and Kissinger added that American diplomacy had proven successful even in holding a meeting with the Arabs during the airlift to Israel. Nor did either man bring up the news that the six Persian Gulf members of OPEC had unilaterally raised the price of oil by 70% and imposed an oil embargo against Israel's allies, chief among them the United States. The use of oil as a political weapon against the United States was just getting started. Arab oil producers had announced that day that they were going to reduce oil production by 5% each month until Israel withdrew from the Arab territory it had occupied since 1967.

By Thursday, October 18, the ceasefire had been reached on the battlefield, and Israeli forces were flooding the Suez Canal and advancing into the West Bank, posing a threat to Egypt's Third Army. Now that a humiliating defeat for Moscow's allies was a real possibility, Brezhnev sent a desperate message to Washington, asking Nixon to send "the US Secretary of State and your closest associate Dr. Kissinger" to Moscow for talks, citing the need for "prompt and effective decisions" due to the "events in the Middle East becoming more and more dangerous." In a sign of how independent he had become from Nixon and how unwilling he was to follow the patterns he had during the first Nixon term, Kissinger told Haig that he thought it would be a "cheap stunt" for the White House to couple the announcement of his trip to Moscow with Nixon's announcement of his proposed compromise in dealing with the White House tapes. Kissinger now felt, "Everyone knows in the Middle East that if they want peace they have to go through us." At the same time, he added, "We can't humiliate the Soviet Union too much." Kissinger told Haig, quite bluntly, "I would not link foreign policy with Watergate. It looks as if he is using foreign policy to cover a domestic thing." Nixon grudgingly consented to split the announcements, saying, "You will regret it for the rest of your life."

Kissinger's visit to Moscow was a watershed in both his own diplomatic style and his relationship with Nixon. It was the final excursion he would take away from the media, and it fell on the same weekend as the infamous "Saturday Night Massacre," when Nixon dismissed Archibald Cox, the Watergate special prosecutor, and Attorney General Elliot Richardson and his deputy William Ruckelshaus resigned. The nation's uproar over Nixon's behaviour dominated media coverage and overshadowed the Middle East, and for the first time, a sizable portion of Congress backed the president's impeachment. Nixon also informed the Soviets of this, which "horrified" Kissinger because it "deprived [him] of any capacity to stall." Kissinger also objected to Nixon's linking of an immediate cease-fire with an overall settlement of the Middle East conflict imposed by the superpowers. Nixon sent Kissinger to Moscow with full authority to negotiate with the Soviets. During their first encounter, it became clear that Kissinger and Brezhnev had similar views on a cease-fire. However, Kissinger objected to Brezhnev using his "full authority" and told the Soviet leader that he would still need to consult the president before reaching any agreements. Kissinger called Haig on an open line to voice his displeasure, but the president's chief of staff told him to "get off my back" after he read the full text of Nixon's instructions and cabled Haig angrily, claiming the president's orders "will totally wreck what little bargaining leverage I still have." Kissinger angrily replied, "What troubles can you possibly have in Washington on a Saturday night? I have troubles of my own."Haig informed him that, following Nixon's decision to remove Cox, "all hell has broken loose."

A cease-fire would be implemented twelve hours after the UN approved the resolution that Kissinger and Brezhnev agreed upon. After that, Kissinger went to Israel. On the verge of total victory, Kissinger was concerned about whether the Israelis would accept the accord. Though he dreaded Soviet assistance if they went too far, he was not opposed to them handing the Arabs an even more crushing defeat. Kissinger assured Ambassador Dinitz that the United States would understand if the Israelis felt they needed some extra time for military dispositions before the cease-fire took effect. Kissinger also informed Golda Meir that the Americans understood that "you have won the war, though at a very high cost," and that "you won't get violent protests from Washington if something happens during the night while I'm flying" after a communications failure in Moscow caused a four-hour delay in informing Israel of the U.S.-Soviet agreement.

Kissinger could have called on Jeremiah, Elijah, and Moses, but the Israelis had no intention of pausing their advance. Kissinger complained to Dinitz once more the following morning about the Israelis breaching the cease-fire and attacking the Third Army. Dinitz attempted to place the blame on the Egyptians, but eventually an irate Kissinger snapped, saying, "Look, Mr. Ambassador, we have been a strong support for you, but we cannot make Brezhnev look like a goddamn fool in front of his colleagues." Kissinger also sarcastically added, "If the Soviets put some divisions in there you will have outsmarted yourselves." Kissinger also revealed that the Soviets were now accusing him of having "gone from Moscow to Tel Aviv to plot with them the overthrow of the whole arrangement we've made," despite his concerns about maintaining détente. The Israelis, he claimed, realised that they could not conduct a war without "an open US supply line," and that even though the Arabs may despise us, or hate us," the US is "the essential ingredient" if they desired a settlement. Everyone must come to us because we are the only ones who can deliver.

Ironically, Haig was right when he surmised that Brezhnev was the one who included the sentence in the Soviet telegram concerning unilateral action. Furious by the ongoing Israeli assaults and appalled by Sadat's plight and Egypt's vulnerability, the Soviet leader had reinforced the message independently. The politburo did not desire a conflict with the United States, and the Soviet military was not ready for combat. The situation subsided nearly as fast as it had emerged. Anwar Sadat agreed to accept a UN force the following day to oversee the cease-fire, and Brezhnev pointedly disregarded the American action, announcing that he was sending seventy Soviet "representatives" to work with a civilian American team to monitor the cease-fire. Now, as Kissinger found out when he convened a news conference to address the alarm, the United States was the one being accused of overreaction. Kissinger downplayed the notion that the US was at war with the USSR in order to defend détente, emphasising that the alert was a "precautionary measure." Nevertheless, reporters focused on whether the US action was a "rational" response, and interrogators suggested that the alert was put in place for domestic political purposes in order to deflect attention from Watergate. Some of the reasons Kissinger had himself stated at the late-night discussion were alluded to in his irate responses. As he had indicated to the NSC the previous evening, he accused the media of seeking to "create a crisis of confidence in foreign policy," implying that it had already created one at home with its investigation of the Watergate affair. Not surprisingly, he also pointed out that the president had not participated in the discussions, even though he emphasised that the decision was the consensus recommendation of senior advisers. He called Nixon later that day to inform him that "Mr. "President, you've triumphed once more," he exclaimed, going on to attack the reporters, including his pals Marvin Kalb, James Reston, and Colman McCarthy, who implied that the alarm was sent for political motives. In an unusual allusion to the 1971 Indo-Pakistani war, Kissinger reminded Nixon that "you were prepared to put forces in as you were prepared to go to nuclear war in Pakistan and that was way before you knew what was going to happen" when he mentioned his intention to hold a press conference the following day.

Although Nixon followed Kissinger's counsel, the outcome was unfavourable. Nixon thought the press conference would give him a chance to celebrate Kissinger's success, but the reporters were still preoccupied with Watergate and the issues brought up by the Saturday Night Massacre. about his choices about Watergate and the dismissal of the special prosecutor, Nixon was both defiant and defensive. However, in response to a question about whether his "Watergate troubles" might have sparked "Soviet thinking about your ability to respond in the Mideast," Nixon emphasised his military actions in the Vietnam War, including his orders for the Christmas bombing, the invasion of Cambodia, and the bombing and mining of North Vietnam. That's "what made Mr. Brezhnev acted as he did," Kissinger said when he called Haig immediately following the end of the news conference, emphasising the contrast with his own strategy of downplaying the confrontation. Brezhnev knew that regardless of the pressures at home, he, Nixon, would do what is right. Kissinger went on, "He has turned it into a massive Soviet back down," publicly humiliating Brezhnev in the process. Kissinger claimed that Nixon ``looked awful'' but requested Haig to try to soften Nixon's statements by calling Dobrynin.

In a momentous occasion, the military leaders of Egypt and Israel convened for the first time on October 28, 1973, to deliberate on the cease-fire and the replenishment of the Egyptian forces. The Middle East might be entering a new era, but clever American diplomacy was needed to take advantage of this chance. The war had brought about a sea change in the Nixon-Kissinger dynamic, with Kissinger now functioning as an effective chief executive while Nixon clung to Kissinger in an attempt to stay alive. In the following months, as Watergate kept erupting and petrol prices shot through the roof, Kissinger pursued a risky, crisis-driven foreign policy whose ingenuity and possible risks would be felt for decades to come.

THE KISSINGER STRATEGY TAKES SHAPE

Kissinger had fresh difficulties when the Middle East's immediate crisis subsided and the cease-fire was established. First and foremost, he had to make sure the brittle cease-fire held. Kissinger was aware of the Golan Heights' continued instability and Israel's desire to destroy Egypt's Third Army. Israel had suffered severe psychological effects from the conflict; the country's 2,668 fatalities matched America's 160,000 fatalities. There was still the risk of a long-term attrition battle. Second, in order to reach a longer-term solution, Kissinger had to initiate talks between the sides, first with the goal of dividing the armed forces. Kissinger wanted to use these negotiations to force the Soviet Union out of the Middle East and show the Arabs and Israelis that peace could only be achieved via American power and diplomacy, in contrast to Nixon's desire for a treaty imposed by the superpowers. Third, despite his desire for them to leave the Middle East, Kissinger remained committed to maintaining the benefits of détente with Russia, particularly in terms of managing the nuclear arms race and averting a potentially catastrophic crisis similar to the one in the Middle East. Fourth, the embargo on Arab oil, which was imposed in reaction to the American resupply of Israel on October 17, persisted. Domestic political pressures would intensify as oil prices skyrocketed, temperatures plummeted, and Americans were forced to stand in lengthy fuel lines and suffer in their homes without heating oil. Nixon constantly pressed Kissinger on this matter in the hopes that lifting the embargo would aid in his ability to win back the public's support. Ultimately, severe tensions within the Western alliance arose in tandem with the pressures and internal political crises. Since the 1950s Suez Crisis, the Yom Kippur War had revealed the deepest differences within the West. For the large American airlift to Israel, the majority of European countries refused to let American planes use their bases. The European countries and Japan, who rely heavily on imported oil, took a strong pro-Arab stance and demanded that Israel withdraw to its 1967 boundaries. France and its foreign minister, Michel Jobert, led this movement. Europe was likewise unprepared for the American nuclear alert, and their loud protests about inadequate consultation reverberated through the foreign offices. With Europeans challenging American leadership and seemingly eager to establish their own Middle East and energy agendas, the "Year of Europe" now seemed hopelessly ironic. America's greatest foreign policy achievement, the Western alliance formed after World War II, was unravelling.

Kissinger tackled this confluence of problems and opportunities with remarkable vigour, acumen, and cunning. In his diary, David Bruce, one of America's patrician diplomats from the early Cold War era who is still serving as an ambassador, encapsulated a key component of Kissinger's strategy: "The spectacle of a fifty-year old German-born Jew, exercising the authority he does in coping with the end of an era complications of universal import elicits my sympathy, dazzles my imagination." Kissinger's "physical and intellectual vigour amaze even those they discomfit." Kissinger came up with a plan after realising how to fit the many parts of the global political jigsaw puzzle to support his interpretation of the interests of the United States as a whole. In addition, he understood that success would only increase his own influence and that he could use his reputation to address these problems. The TV networks began referring to Kissinger as the new "go-between" in negotiations between Israel and the Arab world a few days after the cease-fire. "One thing the Arabs have achieved in this war—regardless of what they lost—is that they've globalised the problem," Kissinger informed Golda Meir as they were arranging a tour to the Arab governments in the region. They have instilled the belief that action is necessary, which we have only prevented through my actions, my journey, and my prestige. Kissinger told the Israelis that he had persuaded the Egyptians that "the Russians can give them arms but only we can give them territory," but that he was now in need of initiating talks in order to relieve some of the pressure on Israel from other quarters. "Russian helicopters going in there, and an enormous crisis which then forces you back anyway" was his "nightmare." Kissinger forced the Israelis to make concessions by posing as Israel's defender.

The atmosphere surrounding Kissinger's sixth visit to China—his first as secretary of state—was influenced by the Middle East's acceptance of the Kissinger Plan. The Chinese greeted him with great enthusiasm, Chairman Mao shaking hands with Kissinger for a considerable amount of time in front of the TV cameras. Kissinger said, "The people who understand our foreign policy best are in

Peking," after the Chinese officials praised the nuclear warning in private. During the summit earlier in the year, Kissinger made it a point to address Brezhnev's menacing remarks about China and offered to provide the Chinese with American intelligence regarding the Soviet threat to their nation. In an attempt to persuade the Chinese that "they want us to accept the desirability of destroying China's nuclear capability or limiting it, rather than the information itself," Kissinger informed them that the Russians had requested American intelligence on China, specifically satellite photographs. Following their discussions, at the banquet, Kissinger gave a toast assuring the Chinese that the new American relationship with China would last "no matter what happens" in Washington. Although Kissinger's remarks were interpreted by reporters as having Watergate motivation, Kissinger assured Nixon in his trip report that the Chinese were on his side. "No more than a breaking of wind," Mao said, displaying his rural humour. Kissinger believed that China and the US had become "tacit allies," with identical perspectives on the USSR and the need for a "strong American world role and defence capability."

In actuality, Kissinger understood that the only way to resolve the issue was to initiate peace talks in the Middle East, since this would demonstrate to the Arab countries that the US was sincerely looking for a solution. "We will have to put pressure on Israel, but if it looks like we did it under duress, we won't even get credit for it," he said to his staff. Kissinger initially tried to call for a Geneva Conference of the superpowers with Israel and the Arab countries under the cover of the UN, with Soviet approval. Kissinger's strategy seems counterintuitive. Kissinger intended to utilise the multilateral conference in Geneva to encourage one-on-one talks between Israel and all of its enemies. The two superpowers would host it, but their intention was to push the Soviets to the background. Kissinger understood that "Soviet cooperation was necessary to convene Geneva: afterward, we would seek to reduce its role to a minimum," as he put it in a later letter. He may have also mentioned that Nixon was a major factor in his support for Geneva, since the president was far more likely than Kissinger to desire to cooperate with the Soviet Union in the Middle East. Kissinger planned an alternative course of action, but the conference gave him the appearance of doing as the president requested.

When it came to Nixon's thoughts and suggestions—the majority of which sprang from the president's belief that a significant victory may diffuse the anger surrounding Watergate—Kissinger was less tactful. "He [Nixon] does that and he is in deep trouble with me," Kissinger said to Brent Scowcroft, the deputy assistant on the National Security Council, when Nixon was thinking about sending a special envoy to Saudi Arabia to try to ease the oil embargo. A move that would present the US as a "supplicant" to the Saudis and "was hardly the best way to convey imperviousness to pressure" was something Kissinger was certain Nixon would "calm down" and that he could convince the president of. When he learned that Nixon had met Dobrynin alone to talk about the Middle East, he responded with equal vehemence. Kissinger informed Haig that these kinds of meetings undermined his diplomatic credentials. It is evident that Kissinger feared that Nixon would present both nations with an alternative understanding of US policy than what Kissinger was attempting to accomplish, especially with reference to Soviet engagement in the process. He expressed dissatisfaction at "flying blind" and made it clear to Haig that he had to make sure "that this sort of thing does not happen again."

Kissinger was adamant about trying to lessen the anti-American forces in Europe and reestablish American leadership of the alliance. The principal foe of Kissinger was Jobert, the foreign minister of France, who promoted an Arab-European dialogue that Kissinger saw as a challenge to his own Middle East policy. Kissinger tried to mimic the oil producers and OPEC in order to oppose Jobert and isolate the French. In a significant address given in December 1973 in London, England, to the esteemed Society of Pilgrims, Kissinger suggested "creating an international consumers group to regulate world demand" for energy. The oil-consuming countries' power in negotiating with the oil producers would be strengthened by the formation of such an "energy action group." Kissinger's idea for an association of energy users was intended to reclaim the initiative for US diplomacy, in addition to calling the Geneva Conference. Europe saw that the Americans had a plan to address both the Middle East situation and the economic difficulties that the Western democracies were confronting.

When the Geneva Conference was called to order on December 21, 1973, it was hailed as a momentous occasion right away. Kissinger persuaded the Israelis, Jordanians, and Egyptians to go, even if the Syrians chose not to go. The Chancellor of NBC stated, "Arabs and Israelis were sitting down together to discuss the prospects for peace for the first time since the creation of the state of Israel." The official event provided an opportunity for strong comments, with the foreign minister of Egypt threatening to go back to war if the discussions failed. Kissinger expressed disappointment that the Saudis had not lifted the oil embargo after the summit opened. He emphasised that while "the atmosphere could not be characterised as one of reconciliation, the parties were careful to keep all doors open" in his report to Nixon. "Your strategy is working well," he continued, expressing his ongoing effort to diffuse Nixon's objections. Being "the only participant who is in close touch with all the parties, the only power that can produce progress, and the only one that each is coming to in order to make that progress" was Kissinger's description of this tactic. This wasn't Nixon's plan; it was an accurate description of his approach.

THE SALZBURG PRESS CONFERENCE AND THE END OF

THE NIXON PRESIDENCY

Kissinger's unquestioning praise did not endure for very long. Even if Kissinger considered the agreement to depart from Syria a real "watershed" event in the Middle East peace process, the Watergate affair had altered the climate in Washington. As the impeachment hearings for the president proceeded, Kissinger's personal shield from criticism began to erode. During his initial press conference upon his return from the area, Kissinger was confronted with a barrage of questions pertaining to his involvement in starting wiretaps on journalists and staff, rather than the Golan Heights. Additionally, he was questioned about his knowledge of the "Plumbers." In the event of a potential perjury probe, a reporter inquired as to whether Kissinger had hired legal representation. "I am not conducting my office as if it were a conspiracy," a furious Kissinger retorted. Kissinger appeared more defensive when he said that this was a "press conference not a cross-examination" and avoided directly answering the question of whether he had "recommended" the wiretaps when the questions about his involvement in the recordings persisted.

Kissinger's point was that his previous responses had obscured the reality of his involvement in both of these matters. Outraged by the bombing in Cambodia leaks, Kissinger complied with the wiretapping gladly, even excitedly, hoping to reassure Nixon of his allegiance. He gave the names of his staff members who had access to the confidential material to FBI director Hoover. Nixon's resolve to undermine Ellsberg by breaking into his psychiatrist's office was influenced by Kissinger's rage at the Pentagon Papers leak and his focus on Ellsberg's psychological fragility. Even though Kissinger may not have been aware of Plumber's activity, it is difficult to trust his claim of total ignorance about them given his strong sensitivity to his position within the Nixon inner circle. Even while he could still claim innocence, Kissinger's defensiveness revealed how closely he was connected to several of the scandals that were endangering Nixon's presidency.

In this instance, Kissinger concluded that a potent offence made for the finest defence. Kissinger accompanied Nixon to the Middle East, and once the trip was finished, he would not wait to answer the claims against him. Before leaving the United States, he spent considerable time practising his arguments with favourable reporters, such as the ABC anchor Howard K. Smith. He also made the decision to have a press conference in Salzburg, Austria, where the presidential party was stopping on route to the Middle East. A sombre and unsmiling Kissinger spoke at "the drawing room of the Kavalier House... in front of the tapestry of a mediaeval forest," during what the TV newscasts called the "strangest press conference ever held by an American Secretary of State." Kissinger worked himself up into a furious and defiant passion, accusing other people of undermining his "honour" and "unnamed sources." Kissinger seemed less defensive and significantly more defiant by focusing on some of the more severe and generally unproven claims that had surfaced. Against the "innuendo" that he and his staff had read transcripts of the wiretaps, which contained "salacious" information about "extramarital affairs or pornographic information," he fiercely defended himself. Kissinger spoke in an almost maudlin way about how he had hoped to "end division" in the United States and that "when the record is written, one may remember that perhaps some lives were saved and that perhaps some mothers can rest more at ease, but I leave that to history." Kissinger also threatened to resign if he was not fully vindicated.

This was a tremendous story, front page news on all the major newspapers and television networks, thanks to Kissinger's stubborn rage and passionate tone. Kissinger's accompanying American ambassador to Germany, Martin Hillenbrand, expected him to remain quite passionate and irritated after he left the press conference to attend a meeting with the German foreign secretary. Rather, Kissinger was "totally calm and looking forward to the meeting," according to Hillenbrand. "I could only give him the highest marks for thespian ability," said Hillenbrand, wryly.

It was a useful act for him. Nixon's hopes of a triumphant tour were dashed by Kissinger's resignation threat, and the president was displeased that his secretary of state was taking centre stage once more. More significantly, it sparked a chorus of bipartisan political endorsement for Kissinger, which highlighted the lack of similar enthusiasm for Nixon. Mike Mansfield, the Senate Democratic leader, pushed Kissinger to continue in his position, while Hubert Humphrey said his pal should just "cool it." Barry Goldwater, a Republican, fiercely backed Kissinger and disparaged his detractors. The Senate Foreign Relations Committee, chaired by J. William Fulbright, expressed his continued confidence in Kissinger, but the committee promptly decided to reconvene hearings to consider the claims against him. Supporting statements were also made by newspaper columnists, such as Joseph Alsop, who questioned if it was really necessary to "hound from office the most admired public servant in the United States." By the weekend, Kissinger was clearly winning the war of public opinion, as seen by the headline "Capital Rallying Around Kissinger" in The New York Times.

As Nixon made his first visit to Damascus as an American president, he was greeted with applause by about a million people in Cairo, mostly caused by Sadat's security forces. An uneasy Kissinger remained in the background. Nixon visited Tel Aviv and spoke with Israeli officials despite having an acute case of phlebitis; yet, he again reflected his differences with Kissinger by expressing greater understanding for the Arab perspective. Even Kissinger was still debating what to do next, whether to pursue an Israeli-Jordanian peace process or stick to his game plan on the Egyptian front. In his memoirs, Kissinger expressed his jealousy of Nixon's attention-seeking ways by stating that Ziegler, the president's press secretary, "defended his notion of Presidential preeminence in news stories with the ferocity of a police dog." The president's waning popularity was not helped by the trip, and Nixon's close circle of advisors started to feel the effects of a kind of deathwatch, which Kissinger subsequently described as the "grim, unspoken backdrop of the journey."

There was another journey to Moscow in the latter days of the Nixon administration, but the atmosphere was substantially different from that of 1972. The government was accused by Senator Henry Jackson of concealing secret agreements struck with the Soviets during the SALT I negotiations. Jackson's ambition for the presidency coincided with his Cold War misgivings about the Soviets. Jackson's accusations, Kissinger retorted angrily, were "false in every detail." Senator Fulbright championed Kissinger's cause and denounced "hawks" such as Jackson for obstructing the possibility of reaching a new strategic armaments accord with the Soviet Union. By stating that any more significant deal would be subject to particular scrutiny in the United States due to the "contentious debate" surrounding Watergate, Kissinger purposefully reduced expectations for the meeting. Kissinger himself was aware that the United States was travelling to Moscow with a number of weapons recommendations that he thought would pose a challenge to the Soviet Union. Despite the considerable asymmetry between the US and Soviet nuclear arsenals, Defense Secretary Schlesinger had vehemently opposed a new SALT agreement. In fact, he had corresponded with Jackson directly, applauding his insistence that any new SALT pact require exact equality in numbers. Kissinger believed that Schlesinger ought to have been fired from the administration for his affiliation with a dissident like Jackson. Nixon begged for greater negotiation flexibility from the defence secretary, but Schlesinger refused to give it to him. Kissinger accused Schlesinger of "patronising" Nixon by assuring the president he had "great forensic skills" and should be able to convince Brezhnev to delay the Soviet MIRV program and accomplish a "major breakthrough." This was an example of the pot calling the kettle black. Although Schlesinger's argument, in Nixon's opinion, "was really an insult to everybody's intelligence and particularly to mine," the president was powerless to persuade his government to support yet another SALT deal.

Kissinger's unquestioning praise did not endure for very long. Even if Kissinger considered the agreement to depart from Syria a real "watershed" event in the Middle East peace process, the Watergate affair had altered the climate in Washington. As the impeachment hearings for the president proceeded, Kissinger's personal shield from criticism began to erode. During his initial press conference upon his return from the area, Kissinger was confronted with a barrage of questions pertaining to his involvement in starting wiretaps on journalists and staff, rather than the Golan Heights. Additionally, he was questioned about his knowledge of the "Plumbers." In the event of a potential perjury probe, a reporter inquired as to whether Kissinger had hired legal representation. "I am not conducting my office as if it were a conspiracy," a furious Kissinger retorted. Kissinger appeared more defensive when he said that this was a "press conference not a cross-examination" and avoided directly answering the question of whether he had "recommended" the wiretaps when the questions about his involvement in the recordings persisted.

Kissinger's point was that his previous responses had obscured the reality of his involvement in both of these matters. Outraged by the bombing in Cambodia leaks, Kissinger complied with the wiretapping gladly, even excitedly, hoping to reassure Nixon of his allegiance. He gave the names of his staff members who had access to the confidential material to FBI director Hoover. Nixon's resolve to undermine Ellsberg by breaking into his psychiatrist's office was influenced by Kissinger's rage at the Pentagon Papers leak and his focus on Ellsberg's psychological fragility. Even though Kissinger may not have been aware of Plumber's activity, it is difficult to trust his claim of total ignorance about them given his strong sensitivity to his position within the Nixon inner circle. Even while he could still claim innocence, Kissinger's defensiveness revealed how closely he was connected to several of the scandals that were endangering Nixon's presidency.

In this instance, Kissinger concluded that a potent offence made for the finest defence. Kissinger accompanied Nixon to the Middle East, and once the trip was finished, he would not wait to answer the claims against him. Before leaving the United States, he spent considerable time practising his arguments with favourable reporters, such as the ABC anchor Howard K. Smith. He also made the decision to have a press conference in Salzburg, Austria, where the presidential party was stopping on route to the Middle East. A sombre and unsmiling Kissinger spoke at "the drawing room of the Kavalier House... in front of the tapestry of a mediaeval forest," during what the TV newscasts called the "strangest press conference ever held by an American Secretary of State." Kissinger worked himself up into a furious and defiant passion, accusing other people of undermining his "honour" and "unnamed sources." Kissinger seemed less defensive and significantly more defiant by focusing on some of the more severe and generally unproven claims that had surfaced. Against the "innuendo" that he and his staff had read transcripts of the wiretaps, which contained "salacious" information about "extramarital affairs or pornographic information," he fiercely defended himself. Kissinger spoke in an almost maudlin way about how he had hoped to "end division" in the United States and that "when the record is written, one may remember that perhaps some lives were saved and that perhaps some mothers can rest more at ease, but I leave that to history." Kissinger also threatened to resign if he was not fully vindicated.

This was a tremendous story, front page news on all the major newspapers and television networks, thanks to Kissinger's stubborn rage and passionate tone. Kissinger's accompanying American ambassador to Germany, Martin Hillenbrand, expected him to remain quite passionate and irritated after he left the press conference to attend a meeting with the German foreign secretary. Rather, Kissinger was "totally calm and looking forward to the meeting," according to Hillenbrand. "I could only give him the highest marks for thespian ability," said Hillenbrand, wryly.

It was a useful act for him. Nixon's hopes of a triumphant tour were dashed by Kissinger's resignation threat, and the president was displeased that his secretary of state was taking centre stage once more. More significantly, it sparked a chorus of bipartisan political endorsement for Kissinger, which highlighted the lack of similar enthusiasm for Nixon. Mike Mansfield, the Senate Democratic leader, pushed Kissinger to continue in his position, while Hubert Humphrey said his pal should just "cool it." Barry Goldwater, a Republican, fiercely backed Kissinger and disparaged his detractors. The Senate Foreign Relations Committee, chaired by J. William Fulbright, expressed his continued confidence in Kissinger, but the committee promptly decided to reconvene hearings to consider the claims against him. Supporting statements were also made by newspaper columnists, such as Joseph Alsop, who questioned if it was really necessary to "hound from office the most admired public servant in the United States." By the weekend, Kissinger was clearly winning the war of public opinion, as seen by the headline "Capital Rallying Around Kissinger" in The New York Times.

As Nixon made his first visit to Damascus as an American president, he was greeted with applause by about a million people in Cairo, mostly caused by Sadat's security forces. An uneasy Kissinger remained in the background. Nixon visited Tel Aviv and spoke with Israeli officials despite having an acute case of phlebitis; yet, he again reflected his differences with Kissinger by expressing greater understanding for the Arab perspective. Even Kissinger was still debating what to do next, whether to pursue an Israeli-Jordanian peace process or stick to his game plan on the Egyptian front. In his memoirs, Kissinger expressed his jealousy of Nixon's attention-seeking ways by stating that Ziegler, the president's press secretary, "defended his notion of Presidential preeminence in news stories with the ferocity of a police dog." The president's waning popularity was not helped by the trip, and Nixon's close circle of advisors started to feel the effects of a kind of deathwatch, which Kissinger subsequently described as the "grim, unspoken backdrop of the journey."

There was another journey to Moscow in the latter days of the Nixon administration, but the atmosphere was substantially different from that of 1972. The government was accused by Senator Henry Jackson of concealing secret agreements struck with the Soviets during the SALT I negotiations. Jackson's ambition for the presidency coincided with his Cold War misgivings about the Soviets. Jackson's accusations, Kissinger retorted angrily, were "false in every detail." Senator Fulbright championed Kissinger's cause and denounced "hawks" such as Jackson for obstructing the possibility of reaching a new strategic armaments accord with the Soviet Union. By stating that any more significant deal would be subject to particular scrutiny in the United States due to the "contentious debate" surrounding Watergate, Kissinger purposefully reduced expectations for the meeting. Kissinger himself was aware that the United States was travelling to Moscow with a number of weapons recommendations that he thought would pose a challenge to the Soviet Union. Despite the considerable asymmetry between the US and Soviet nuclear arsenals, Defense Secretary Schlesinger had vehemently opposed a new SALT agreement. In fact, he had corresponded with Jackson directly, applauding his insistence that any new SALT pact require exact equality in numbers. Kissinger believed that Schlesinger ought to have been fired from the administration for his affiliation with a dissident like Jackson. Nixon begged for greater negotiation flexibility from the defence secretary, but Schlesinger refused to give it to him. Kissinger accused Schlesinger of "patronising" Nixon by assuring the president he had "great forensic skills" and should be able to convince Brezhnev to delay the Soviet MIRV program and accomplish a "major breakthrough." This was an example of the pot calling the kettle black. Although Schlesinger's argument, in Nixon's opinion, "was really an insult to everybody's intelligence and particularly to mine," the president was powerless to persuade his government to support yet another SALT deal.

Chapter 5: No Longer Indispensable

FOLLOWING THE "HALLOWEEN MASSACRE" OF OCTOBER 1975, WHEN PRESIDENT GERALD FORD Sacked Secretary of Defence James Schlesinger and CIA Director William Colby, as well as removing Kissinger's role as national security adviser, rumours spread that Kissinger would quit as secretary of state soon. ABC's diplomatic correspondent, Barrie Dunsmore, began a report contrasting Kissinger's position after the Syria disengagement agreement, when he was "Super K," at the "height of his career," and "everybody's favourite," with his current situation, where he had become "everybody's favourite target." Dunsmore compiled an impressive list of attacks on Kissinger, including the Senate Intelligence Committee report criticising Kissinger's role in the Chilean government's overthrow; congressional testimony by former chief of naval operations Admiral Elmo Zumwalt, who accused Kissinger of lying about Soviet violations of the SALT treaty; and James Schlesinger's characterization of détente as weakness towards the Soviet Union. When Dunsmore weighed these factors against Kissinger's success in the Middle East and strong connections with the Russians and Chinese, he concluded that Kissinger was now "more popular abroad than he was in the United States." The true meaning of the "so-called Halloween Massacre," Dunsmore intoned, was that Henry Kissinger was "no longer indispensable," adding that "while the thought of Gerald Ford being without Kissinger may have been unthinkable only a few months ago, many people are thinking about it today, including Henry Kissinger." The "Kissinger is about to resign" story was covered every few weeks for the next several months, always based on the best confidential sources.

Although Kissinger's stint as Secretary of State under Gerald Ford was contentious, Dunsmore's prognosis of Kissinger's downfall proved to be far too optimistic. Even if he was not "indispensable," Kissinger remained a prominent role in American foreign policy until the conclusion of the Ford administration, aggressively attempting to settle the Rhodesian civil war, preserving the SALT agreement with the Soviet Union, and formulating fresh Middle East ideas. Despite ideological criticism from both ends of the political spectrum, Kissinger strove to manage and adapt to the shifting tides of American public opinion, and to persuade that opinion to keep Ford as president.

DEFENDING DÉTENTE: THE JACKSON-VANIK AMENDMENT AND THE VLADIVOSTOK CONFERENCE

Kissinger firmly believed in the goals of détente, both for their domestic political appeal (as demonstrated by Nixon's landslide) and for their foreign policy utility—reducing the threat of nuclear war, slowing the arms race, and stabilising the relationship between the superpowers in ways that promoted trust and reduced the risk of armed conflict. All of these justifications for détente were significantly more important to Kissinger than issues like Jewish emigration or the repression of Soviet dissidents. Kissinger rationalised the trade-off by claiming that the Soviet Union will "evolve" or develop internally in "an environment of decreasing international tensions." Kissinger saw this as yet another reason to maintain détente and avoid Jackson's legislative recommendations. Kissinger collaborated with his Soviet counterpart behind the scenes to assist Jewish emigration, which surged after 1969. Kissinger followed Ford's lead in trying for a compromise with Jackson, despite his firm belief that "quiet diplomacy" was more effective than loud demands. Recognising the domestic politics at play, he may have believed that by collaborating with Jackson, the Democratic nominee at the time, they could defuse the problem before the 1976 election. In September, Kissinger told the Senate Foreign Relations Committee that the Soviets had assured him that the education exit tax "was no longer being collected." We've been guaranteed that it will not be used again." He went on to say that the volume of Jewish emigration was increasing and that "we are now moving towards an understanding that should significantly diminish the obstacles to emigration and ease the hardship of prospective emigrants." Both the Soviet foreign minister, Andrei Gromyko, and Dobrynin had privately told Ford and Kissinger that their government would give them assurances that they would allow 50,000 Jews to leave the Soviet Union each year.

Kissinger and Jackson eventually agreed to exchange letters on their accord with Ford's support. Kissinger's letter to Jackson reported on the administration's commitments regarding stopping harassment and treating emigrants equitably. It avoided exact estimates but assumed that "the rate of emigration from the USSR would begin promptly from the 1973 level and would continue to rise to correspond to the number of applicants." Jackson's letter was far more detailed, establishing a benchmark figure of sixty thousand emigrants as "a minimum standard of initial compliance." On October 18, 1974, Kissinger and Jackson, along with the president, Senator Jacob Javits of New York, and Congressman Charles Vanik of Ohio, celebrated the signing of the Jackson-Vanik Amendment, which barred states from receiving most-favoured-nation status if they restricted their citizens' emigration rights. Kissinger sat in the background, curiously quiet, as Javits praised the law as "historic... like Moses leading his people out of slavery." Jackson lauded the accord as the administration's "first major effort in bipartisan policy," for which Ford "deserved a lot of credit." Despite the event's joyous tone, Jackson was enraged that Brezhnev did not help with "that foul statement." He was responding to Brezhnev's recent remarks to American business executives that imposing "utterly and unacceptable stipulations" on US-Soviet trade were attempts at "interference in internal affairs." Jackson rejected it as Soviet domestic posturing, praising the accord as a "historic understanding in the area of human rights" and declaring, "There has been a complete turnaround on the basic points that are contained in the two letters." The same point was made by all three network newscasts, with NBC's John Chancellor declaring that the accord amounted to a Soviet "cave-in to American congressmen led by Senator Jackson."

While such Machiavellian plotting is feasible, another explanation, reflecting both Kissinger's calculations and his hubris, seems more likely. Kissinger was on his way to Moscow to prepare for the summit conference in Vladivostok. His primary focus had shifted to the prospect of a SALT II agreement, which Jackson and his allies would reject. On his arrival in Moscow, Kissinger was certain that as the most admired man in America and the "incontestable captain of diplomacy," as Dobrynin referred to him, he could minimise the MFN problem and reach a deal on SALT. When Brezhnev started their Moscow talks by criticising the Jackson-Vanik Amendment and Jackson's statements, Kissinger pounded the table and declared that Jackson's "manner is as humiliating for me as it is for you" and that the "press is saying that Kissinger has been defeated by Jackson." Then, in a dramatic manner, Kissinger exclaimed, "I'm as angry as you are," before storming out of the room. This, like his press conference in Salzburg, was another example of Kissinger's theatrical approach to diplomacy. His plan was to utilise Jackson to persuade the Soviets to reach an arrangement with him. Kissinger wanted Brezhnev to perceive him as a key partner against Senator Jackson and "the individuals and groups that oppose the betterment of Soviet-American relations," as Brezhnev put it.

For the Soviets, Kissinger personified détente, arguing that he was both its most essential symbol and best champion. After his walkout, he told Brezhnev that his personal popularity was at an all-time high of 80%, "which is extraordinary for a non-elected official." "Or an elected official," Dobrynin generously added, without any apparent scepticism, "number one in history." Kissinger recalled how he had just attempted to engage Jackson in a discussion about détente, but Jackson "was afraid of a confrontation." Kissinger informed the

Russians that he was not "considered a partisan political figure," which meant he couldn't criticise Jackson or play a direct role in the current midterm election campaign. Kissinger enticed the Soviets by claiming that if they "came to a SALT agreement in principle in Vladivostok" and Jackson criticised it, Kissinger would be free to tour the country defending the accord and criticising Jackson. When Brezhnev inquired about how the Soviets could assist, Kissinger replied, "The best way is if you and I are on the same side and Jackson is on the other." When Brezhnev said, "I agree," Kissinger responded with resounding confidence, "Then we'll almost certainly win."

Kissinger attempted to address Brezhnev's other objections in order to move to the SALT negotiations after establishing that they were, for all practical reasons, on the same side in this conflict with Jackson. He defended the trade pact as the "best we can do," but admitted that Brezhnev's criticisms were valid. He stated his own stance on the proposed European Security Conference, criticising it substantially but anticipating that the remaining difficulties would be settled quickly and the accord would be signed in early 1975. In defending his shuttle diplomacy in the Middle East, Kissinger managed to elicit a smile from the normally reserved Gromyko by implying that Anwar Sadat was playing a "double game" with the Americans and the Soviets, attempting to extract more economic and military aid from both countries while pitting them against each other. Kissinger likewise kept a straight face when he told Brezhnev, "Especially in the Middle East, I think neither of us can gain a permanent advantage at the expense of the other, and any attempt by either of us to do so is going to be entirely futile." Although his Soviet counterparts were unlikely to be duped, they let it pass. Brezhnev then asked what Americans meant when they said they "must be second to none in terms of strength," and what Kissinger believed about the potential of an atomic war between their two countries. The Soviet leader then called a halt to the talks for the day to give the American secretary of state time to mull over his difficult questions, stating, "On that thought, I wish you pleasant dreams."

Kissinger joked that he would ask Washington for advice on how to respond to Brezhnev. He actually requested a presidential message of support. Kissinger told Ford that he believed Brezhnev was sceptical about Ford's personal support for the secretary. Whether it was a sign of Kissinger's perennial insecurity or a ploy to get Brezhnev to talk more concretely about SALT, Ford sent a strong message of support, telling the Soviet leader that he had authorised "Secretary Kissinger to discuss with you the cardinal elements of a new agreement, which we will address in our forthcoming meeting." The next day, Brezhnev brandished Ford's wire at Kissinger while listening to him discuss the "objective realities of American defence planning." Brezhnev argued once more that the US was pursuing nuclear dominance. Kissinger denied this charge and then personalised the situation by declaring, "Any analysis of the US scene would show that I alone have kept the possibility of an agreement open." Every proposition I've presented to you in the previous year has been met with hostility from the majority of the US administration."

Kissinger added an essential cautionary note to his cable informing Ford of the Soviet surrender, reminding him that the Soviet plan "would be shredded" by the Defence Department and leaked to the press and Jackson before "we can shape it." To do this, Kissinger asked Ford not to reveal any specific information to Schlesinger until he returned to Washington. Gromyko also delivered Kissinger a letter, "written not on Foreign Ministry stationery but on plain brownish paper," rejecting the letters Kissinger had exchanged with Jackson over the trade bill. The Russians were engaging in their own version of linkage, providing concessions in the SALT talks in the hope that it would drive Ford and Kissinger to push back against Jackson on trade, most-favoured-nation status, and even Jewish emigration. Kissinger chose a different approach, withholding the existence of the Gromyko letter from all but the president until after Vladivostok, thinking that an agreement there would persuade the Soviets to back down. The Soviet reaction to Jackson's pressure, Kissinger told Ford, "shows that what I predicted and warned Jackson about for months has now happened." Despite his fears that the Soviets would publicise the Gromyko letter, Kissinger felt they would support the trade deal and let emigration to continue "for fear of strengthening Jackson."

Kissinger was engaged in a complex game, and the Soviets were no longer cooperating. He hoped that the Soviets would see it as in their best interests to swallow the Jackson-Vanik Amendment's "interference" in their internal affairs, the degree to which it restricted how they controlled their own people, in order to help Ford and Kissinger politically win Senate approval for the SALT II treaty. Kissinger believed that the Soviets would follow Kissinger's advice on both the trade bill and SALT because they feared strengthening Henry Jackson politically. It was a bet on Kissinger's part, motivated by his overbearing feeling of his significance to the Soviets, and it underestimated Brezhnev's willingness to accept foreign influence over Soviet internal practices, as permitted by the Jackson-Vanik Amendment.

In the brief period between Kissinger's visit to Moscow and the Vladivos- tok summit, Kissinger attempted to persuade Ford that his evaluation of the Soviet offer on SALT was correct, and that he was vital to any agreement. He emphasised détente politics, believing that it divided Democrats between the Jackson and Kennedy wings, and that if Ford abandoned détente, the Democrats would re-unite in opposition to the government. As the summit approached, Kissinger offered Ford a pep talk, advising him not to worry about parallels to Nixon because Nixon "was a poor negotiator," and that all he needed to do was "act confident." When Kissinger urged that Ford "show you had an option and instinct to go to the right," Ford said, "I have a tough and bombastic side." "I wouldn't do that," Kissinger instantly corrected the president. I'd show him a little bit and then throttle it. Maintain a tough but friendly demeanour." Ford's uneasiness was palpable when he told Kissinger that he didn't want any private meetings with Brezhnev unless Kissinger was there because "we are a team." He went on to say, "If you see things heading the wrong way, don't hesitate to set it straight."

Ford was delighted with the "framework" deal made in Vladivostok, even if his spokeswoman overstated the magnitude of the achievement. Kissinger described the deal as an opportunity to "break the back of the arms race," with a new treaty likely to be signed during Brezhnev's anticipated visit in June 1975. Kissinger admitted that many technical concerns remained, particularly those concerning verification. He went on to say that there were still difficult negotiations ahead that "could fail," but that he believed they were "well down the road." Reporters remarked that Kissinger's "exuberant manner," more than his actual words, led some to believe that a deal was on the horizon, while others were sceptical of what was simply an agreement to pursue an accord. Kissinger did not return to the US with Ford, but instead travelled to Beijing, where he continued to play the triangular diplomacy game, keeping the Soviets concerned about the American connection with China and the Chinese concerned about his interactions with the Soviet Union. Despite his belief that the Vladivostok conference gave him "leverage" with Beijing, Kissinger discovered that the Chinese were not cooperating. The Chinese proved more difficult than Kissinger had experienced on previous trips from the start of the discussions, when they invited Kissinger's adversary, Defence Secretary Schlesinger, to come for a visit. They expressed dissatisfaction with the discussions' location in Vladivostok, a region of the Soviet Union where Chinese had previously resided. They also assailed the détente policy with a zeal that, as Kissinger put it, would have pleased the "neoconservatives at Commentary." The Chinese were developing a more sophisticated grasp of American politics, and they recognised some of the disappointment with détente in the US, symbolised by figures such as Schlesinger. Kissinger's attempt to strike a balance between the two communist nations was failing. This was reinforced when his interlocutor on this tour was not his favourite Zhou Enlai, but Deng Xiaoping, whom Kissinger regarded as a "nasty little man." Furthermore, Kissinger was not afforded the normal honour of meeting Chairman Mao during this visit. It foreshadowed the difficulties that were to come in the one diplomatic relationship in which Kissinger took an almost parental concern.

Kissinger returned from China in early December to testify in support of the trade measure, which was in risk of failing to pass before Congress adjourned on December 20. Kissinger did not reveal the Gromyko letter to the committee, but he did reiterate that the Soviet Union had not promised a precise number of emigration. Kissinger made an impassioned case for the bill, claiming that its rejection would be a "disastrous blow" to America's worldwide standing. The bill passed the Senate a little more than a week later, but while it was being reconciled with the House version in conference committee, the Soviet Union publicly released the Gromyko letter, stating unequivocally that they would not accept what they saw as the "interference in internal affairs" of the Jackson-Vanik Amendment. The report about the "Soviet rejection of the trade bill" headlined the evening news on all three networks, with Senator Jackson defending his work, claiming that the Russian action was for their own internal consumption and that he was still convinced they would honour the pact. Kissinger told Ford that he now feared the Russians would reject the MFN agreement, and that the $300 million given through the Export-Import Bank was not worth the sacrifice they were making by agreeing to emigration. Kissinger stated that Dobrynin told him that they saw "a shift of Executive Power to the Congress," suggesting that agreements with the Ford administration were no longer regarded as credible or likely to be ratified. Later that evening, when Kissinger called Dobrynin, he personalised the situation again, telling the Soviet envoy that he had discovered that this was the start of a Kremlin attack on him that was completely unfair, because Kissinger had "been trying to defend the Soviet point of view." The Soviets did not relent, and Kissinger's hope to convince the Soviets to trust him and accept the trade bill as a necessary evil of American politics failed.

As the year drew to a finish, the news for Kissinger did not get much better. Both Ford and Kissinger were concerned that what Ford dubbed "a new generation of wildass Democrats' ' in the recently elected Congress were trying to undercut and undermine presidential power, especially over foreign policy. The newly minted members of the "fighting ninety-fourth [Congress] were exultant in the muscle they had used to bring a President down, willing and able to challenge the Executive as well as its own Congressional hierarchy, intense over morality in government [and] extremely sensitive to press and public pressures." The trade law was simply the tip of the iceberg, as Congress was more determined to reestablish its power against the "Imperial Presidency." The cessation of military help to Turkey was a forerunner of this aggressiveness, but the legislative role also reflected the fracturing of the "Cold War consensus' ' and a willingness to question the trade-offs presidents had made in the name of national security. Representative Donald Fraser, who chaired the House Foreign Affairs Subcommittee on International Organizations and Movements, held hearings in 1973 and 1974 that highlighted human rights atrocities among American allies such as Greece, Chile, and South Vietnam. Kissinger warned Ford, "In the name of human rights, they will undermine national security." In what might have been one of his most tone-deaf bits of advice, Kissinger wanted the former congressman Ford "to go to the people against the Congress," pledging that he would join him, and talk about "the Executive-Legislative relationship."

THE BITTER TASTE OF FAILURE: THE SINAI NEGOTIATIONS AND THE FALL OF SAIGON

Gerald Ford began his first State of the Union address on January 15, 1975, by informing Americans that the "State of the Union is not good." The recession had put millions out of work, high oil prices had exacerbated inflation, and the federal budget deficit was expanding at an unprecedented rate. Ford's speech focused on domestic issues, but near the end, he lauded recent international policy and warned, "This is not the moment for the American people to turn inward." While pledging to work with Congress on foreign policy, he also stated, "We cannot rigidly limit the President's ability to act in legislation." Even if "intended for the best motives and purposes," such congressional limits, Ford said, "can have the opposite result, as we have seen most recently in our trade relations with the Soviet Union." The polite remark to the Jackson-Vanik measure's rejection demonstrated Ford's moderation in dealing with Congress. Kissinger was considerably harsher. He told one interviewer that "all Western democracies are currently suffering from a crisis of authority," and his pessimism about the future of the American political system was one of Washington's worst-kept secrets. Kissinger was not alone in his feelings, as Watergate, the oil crisis, and the Western democracies' economic problems sparked widespread alarm. The Trilateral Commission, a nongovernmental organisation formed by David Rockefeller to bring leaders from the United States, Europe, and Japan together, produced a report titled The Crisis of Democracy, which emphasised the challenges of governance in Western democracies.

In the January 1975 atmosphere, Henry Kissinger needed success, and resuming his step-by-step diplomacy in the Middle East could deliver it. Americans regarded the Middle East as both the most perilous region of the globe and the most important to the American economy. Even when Kissinger assured Ford, "The American Jews will oppose you in 1976, because they think you will move in 1977 and with a new party they will have a chance at a better deal," Ford did not need much convincing. Ford predicted that "by next year, energy and the economy will be in better shape," and that doing things one step at a time was the "responsible course." "Only Sadat can make the concessions," Kissinger told Ford, "and he will only do it to you or me." Kissinger used a news conference on January 28 to declare that he would soon embark on "an exploratory trip to the Middle East," with the goal of meeting with "all of the major participants." Despite his efforts to temper expectations, he indicated his own view that the interests "of Egypt, for the return of some territory, and of Israel, for some progress towards peace, can be reconciled."

Kissinger saw the Israeli-Egyptian conflict as the only aspect of the Middle East complex that could be resolved. Kissinger had wanted to follow Syria's pullout with a deal with Jordan, but at the Rabat meeting in October 1974, Arab leaders recognised the Palestine Liberation Organisation as the representation of West Bank Palestinians. The PLO's backing for terrorism rendered it politically viable as a negotiation partner, according to both Israel and a large portion of the American people. Syria had been extensively rearmed by the Soviet Union, and it demanded that the Geneva Conference be reopened, as well as an Israeli return to its 1967 lines. The rising violence along the Lebanese border, with Israel hitting Palestinian militants, added to the sensation that the region was on fire. Kissinger informed the Washington Special Actions Group that he believed there was a prospect of a Soviet invasion in Syria to push Israel back to its 1967 borders. If the US considered bringing in military forces to assist Israel, CIA Director William Colby remarked, "we could write off the entire Arab world." The chairman of the Joint Chiefs of Staff, General George Brown, stated, "It would tear the country apart." Kissinger responded, "That's exactly my nightmare." "If the Arabs win, with Soviet support, and we do nothing," he told the group, "we've had it."

As negative as Kissinger sounded about the future of the Middle East in general, he was rather hopeful about the success of his shuttle diplomacy. Congress would be debating a large military and economic aid package for Israel, and, as Kissinger put it, "you can't be willing to pay $3 billion for a stalemate." Kissinger was also certain that the threat of returning to the Geneva Conference would frighten the Israelis. He assumed that the Israeli government, led by Yitzhak Rabin, recognised that "their specific terms are less important than the continuation of this process—and they will have to take what they can get." Kissinger, on the other hand, was visiting the Middle East for the first time after becoming the target of domestic criticism. Senator Jackson contended that Kissinger's secrecy during the final round of trade negotiations with the Soviets contributed to the failure of the deal. On a more personal level, Nixon's former assistant Charles Colson was freed from prison in late January and began giving interviews. Among Colson's allegations was that President Nixon saw Kissinger as "unstable" during the Vietnam peace talks and was concerned about Gerald Ford's capacity to control Kissinger. Kissinger responded in an interview before departing for the Middle East, lamenting how foreign policy had been "insulated" from criticism during Watergate, and how the attacks on him now "were a new experience."

Kissinger began his "exploratory" tour in Israel, where the realities of Israel's severely divided and disturbed political environment became clear. Kissinger immediately saw that his attempt to use the Geneva Conference as a threat would backfire, because members in Israel's government saw Geneva as "an opportunity to maintain the current impasse." Kissinger also acknowledged that Israel's demand that Egypt formally agree "to end all acts of belligerency" could be too much for Sadat to accept in the current situation. Kissinger's encounter in Egypt was "considerably more relaxed" than his meeting in Tel Aviv, and he felt Sadat would "do his best" to negotiate an agreement. Kissinger discovered Syrian President Bashar al-Assad resolved to "cause problems for Egypt both internally and in the Arab world if Egypt went it alone," but he believed he could manage the Syrian leader if he could produce another successful Israeli disengagement for Egypt. Kissinger maintained his optimism, telling reporters that the odds of another accord were fifty-fifty at best, a calculation that undervalued his true feelings. Kissinger, unfortunately, miscalculated Israel's willingness to sacrifice important territory, including Ras Sudr and the Abu Rudeis oil fields, for a simple non-belligerency vow from Sadat. Israel was prepared to drive a considerably harsher bargain for domestic political reasons.

Kissinger returned to the United States and briefed Ford on his trip in a way that emphasised his personal importance while downplaying the risks. He complained to the president about the Israeli government's and Prime Minister Rabin's weakness, as evidenced by his statement, "I had to have lunch with the Cabinet to win them over." He told Ford, in words reminiscent of how he once described South Vietnam, "You can't imagine the monomania, the hysteria in Israel." There is no sense of thankfulness. They demand that we put our entire policy in their hands." When Ford questioned Kissinger whether he still thought "Israel was setting us up," the secretary of state said Rabin wanted a deal. He went on to say, "But they are in such a difficult domestic situation they could even prefer to go to Geneva and be raped." Kissinger made a point of briefing congressional leaders and American Jewish leaders in more formal terminology. While the US may eventually agree to return to the Geneva Conference, he informed both groups that "it makes an enormous difference under what conditions we go." Returning to Geneva with another successful accord would assist to make the case that "moderation pays" and reinforce those forces in the face of more radical groups. Kissinger also lobbied with Jewish leaders for support for "executive authority" over Congress. He lamented the current political climate, saying, "There is a malaise here." The Jewish leaders informed him that they backed his attempts at incremental diplomacy and found solace in his response to a question, "I won't break any world records to go to Geneva."

Kissinger returned to the Middle East in early March, certain that he would reach another disengagement agreement, bolstering the Ford administration against an increasingly assertive Congress. President Ford connected his personal prestige to Kissinger's mission, greeting him at the airport and delegating complete negotiating authority to him. The rough concept of an agreement was discussed broadly— Israeli withdrawal from two major routes in Sinai, Mitla and Giddi, as well as the Egyptian oil fields there, in exchange for some form of Egyptian pledge of non-aggression. Even if these prerequisites appeared to be met, Kissinger learned that Israel's resistance was far greater than he had imagined. Outside events had a role once again. The news was dominated by a horrific terrorist attack at Tel Aviv's Savoy Hotel. Kissinger had Ford immediately cable Prime Minister Rabin, saying, "We cannot allow this act of terrorism to achieve its goal—the disruption and collapse of our current peace efforts." Kissinger acknowledged that he was attempting to persuade the Israelis to offer "a generous counterproposal which could convince Sadat of their seriousness," rather than a "rigid" point-by-point analysis of each topic in any deal. It was a strategy that demanded a high level of faith in their mediator, and Kissinger personalised the negotiations in startling ways. "The impact on our international situation could not be more serious," Kissinger warned Israeli leaders. "From the Shah to Western Europe, from the Soviet Union to Japan it will be hard to explain why the United States failed to move a country of less than three million totally dependent on it in the face of Egyptian proposals which seem extremely generous to them."95 Kissinger, whose belief in the interconnection of world events was crucial to his worldview, became even more frantic for success as he saw America being challenged around the world. Kissinger attempted to scare Tel Aviv as its position solidified, insisting on a written pledge of non-belligerence from Sadat. He wrote a note for Ford to write to Rabin, stating that "the failure to achieve an agreement is bound to have far-reaching effects in the area and on our relations." It didn't work, and Kissinger's sixteen-day peace trip to the Middle East ended in "shambles," according to Tom Snyder, the anchor of NBC Nightly News on Sundays.

Kissinger expressed grief in public about the breakdown of the talks, emphasising his exhaustion and weariness. The television coverage showed him visiting with former Prime Minister Golda Meir and then speaking at the airport before leaving, his voice breaking with emotion as he thanked Rabin for his friendship. Before leaving, he privately told the Israeli cabinet that it was "totally out of the question" for the US to resume bilateral diplomacy and that the Geneva negotiations must resume. Kissinger offered a particularly bleak picture for Israelis, telling them that this was "another missed opportunity" and that there was a "good chance" that another conflict would erupt within the next year. When Foreign Minister Yigal Allon challenged him to resume diplomacy in a few weeks, Kissinger personalised the issue, telling Allon, "Because I am no longer the figure who mesmerises them in the Arab world, because in every area the United States is no longer a country that one has to take seriously." As the discussion came to an end, he became philosophical, agreeing with Rabin that this was like a Greek tragedy: "Each side, following the laws of its own nature, reaches an outcome that was perfectly foreseeable."

This was not the way he spoke in Washington. When he reported to President Ford, he was even more enraged, even dismissive of Israelis, telling the president, "I am Jewish." How can I desire this? I've never seen such cold-blooded manipulation of American national interests." He cautioned Ford that the Israelis would "get what they want from Congress and by-pass you," maybe by playing "the Jackson game with the Soviet threat." Without arms, you weaken an ally; with arms, they gain complete freedom." Kissinger used the domestic political allusion on purpose, fearing that Jackson's courtship of American Jews would link his anti-détente efforts with criticism of Kissinger's Middle East diplomacy. Kissinger, like Nixon, mocked Ford when he said, "Israel doesn't think they have to be afraid of you." Ford's firm response, "They will find out," signalled the start of the "reassessment" that Ford had threatened, and Kissinger made certain to convey to the media that "if I were an Israeli, I'd be nervous."

Kissinger desired a tough policy, "a cooling of relations with Israel—which should be friendly but correct," in order to reestablish American leadership in the region, despite his belief that "step-by-step is dead" and that the US should "consider whether we and the Soviet Union shouldn't take a global approach." However, as the reconsideration of Israel began, Kissinger was confronted with another disaster: the inevitable collapse of the American-backed regimes in Cambodia and South Vietnam. He proceeded to the National Security Council meeting after leaving a meeting with congressional leadership, where he got bipartisan statements of support for his Middle East endeavours. He sat there as his aide, William Hyland, explained the chaotic departure of South Vietnamese forces as President Thiu intended to establish a new defensive line along the country's southern border. "What I want to know is how this all happened," Kissinger said flatly after Hyland reported, "We have no idea whatsoever what [Thiu's] supply situation is."

As the final tragedy of Indochina unfolded over the next six weeks, Kissinger's mood shifted from intense anger and resentment at congressional opponents of any further assistance to the South Vietnamese, to defensiveness about his personal role in the tragedy, and finally to a resigned attempt to move America beyond Vietnam. The issue's internal politics, both past and future, were never far from his mind. On March 26, 1975, he gave a press conference in which he made an impassioned call for aid to South Vietnam, describing it as a "moral commitment" that would define "what kind of people we are." It was unusual for Kissinger to utilise moral rhetoric when discussing a foreign policy subject. Although he did not resurrect President Eisenhower's analogy of Southeast Asian nations collapsing like dominoes to the Communists, Kissinger cautioned that failing to intervene would have severe ramifications for the United States. The country might lose allies, see the balance of power tilt against it, and see foes encouraged to target American interests. He challenged, and evidently irritated, Congress and Democrats by claiming that denying aid would "deliberately destroy an ally."

Kissinger's unorthodox use of the French experience shaped his thinking in other ways as well. He now instructed Ford, as he had previously advised Nixon, to do "what De Gaulle did with Algeria—be as tough as nails and don't give ground anywhere." If we are challenged, we must be tough." Kissinger had long liked how De Gaulle had made the French retreat from Algeria appear to be an act of policy by the French, rather than a surrender to the Algerian revolutionaries, in part through his speech and manner. He continued with the most famous British statesman after mentioning the French leader. He advised the president to take a harsh stance while dealing with Congress, saying, "You need a Churchillean posture now." The counsel ran counter to Ford's instincts and those of his political advisers, who urged him to be more accommodating to Congress and distance himself from the Vietnam War. Kissinger initially won, and Ford delivered a powerful speech to Congress on April 10, 1975, begging for $722 million in military and humanitarian aid for South Vietnam. "There was not one clap of applause" for the speech in Congress, with two members even storming out in disgust. Kissinger remained defiant, telling Ford that the Democrats "will have no issue on Vietnam," because they "got us into it." Congress would only contribute funds for the evacuation of 6,000 Americans and "some" South Vietnamese, and even this gesture was contentious. Concerned about "pulling the plug" too soon and causing panic among the Vietnamese, Kissinger continued to plead for help, intending to set clear political boundaries. "Indochina is gone, but we will make them pay for it," he assured Brent Scowcroft. In my entire statement today, I mentioned Congress twenty-five times." Senator Henry Jackson claimed that Nixon's letters to President Thiu promising military action if North Vietnam violated the Paris agreements constituted a "secret" pact. Kissinger denied this. "You know what agony we were going through to get out of that war," Kissinger admitted to Scotty Reston. Everyone wanted us to leave; public opinion was that we should leave immediately. People believe we had a golden opportunity to reach an agreement." What Kissinger refused to recognise was that the "decent interval" he had anticipated between the deal and the eventual fall of South Vietnam was approaching with alarming speed, and that there was no way to stop it.

President Ford delivered a speech at Tulane University on April 23, declaring that the Vietnam War was "a war that is finished as far as America is concerned." The audience's standing ovation and passionate reaction turned Ford's remark into a significant news item, especially after Ford responded to an inquiry about whether Kissinger had any involvement in drafting the speech by stating, "No. "Not at all." "This we don't need," Kissinger angrily informed Ford, but it was evident that the president saw the trend of public mood. Kissinger told sympathetic journalists that, while he was aware that there were people around Ford who wanted Kissinger's influence "diminished," he was staying with the administration "for two reasons—it is not fair to pass along the problems I now have, and, second, I am trying to rally what can be rallied."

Even before Saigon fell, Kissinger had prepared with NBC News president Herbert Schlosser for a four-day appearance on the Today show to defend American foreign policy and his own role as a primary architect of that policy. Ford was excited about the prospect, telling Kissinger that it "burns me up" when people focused on possible differences between the president and his secretary of state. Barbara Walters, the interviewer, had become acquainted with Kissinger, and her demeanour was polite and courteous. Kissinger defended the Ford administration's policies as well as his own personal role in such a relaxed setting. While admitting that Vietnam was a "significant setback," Kissinger justified the administration's rescue of thousands of Vietnamese citizens as part of America's "national duty." He emphasised that it was the Nixon administration that discovered and withdrew 550,000 American soldiers from Vietnam, and he deflected a clumsy question from Walters about the "decent interval" by denying that there were "any very vocal statements" in 1973 suggesting that it was only a "matter of time" before the North Vietnamese took over the South. He restated his own story of why Saigon fell, emphasising the impact of Watergate and congressional cuts in aid and constraints on US military action to implement the Paris agreements, but he allowed, "We probably would have done nothing anyway."

When the conversation went to the Soviet Union, Kissinger admitted that the Soviets provided the munitions for the North Vietnamese advance, making the takeover "possible," but he emphasised that "the refusal of American arms [made the conquest of South Vietnam] inevitable." Kissinger argued vehemently for détente, claiming that "we have certain interests in common, such as the prevention of general nuclear war, such as limiting conflict in areas where both of us could get directly involved." "Détente has never meant the absence of competition," he emphasised, contradicting how he previously phrased it during the heady days of the first Nixon-Brezhnev meetings. Kissinger also offered a less broad and global reading of South Vietnam's fall than he had previously articulated, telling Walters, "We might have perceived it more in Vietnamese terms rather than as the outward thrust of global conspiracy." Kissinger was attempting to position himself as an advocate of a policy that would "gear American commitments to American capabilities and necessities," a realisation of American power's limitations. The issue with this approach is that his personalising of the process frequently meant that he wanted to engage American power while he was in control of it, and Congress had thwarted that dynamic. When Walters pressed Kissinger on the charge "that you are gloomy about what you see as the decline and erosion of the free world," he admitted, "It is partly true," and went on to say that "in many countries Marxist ideologies and perceptions of the world, which are contrary to our values, are gaining strength."

President Ford invited Kissinger to be a member of his 1976 election campaign the following Monday, May 12, at their morning meeting. Kissinger enthusiastically responded, assuring Ford that this election would be "one of the most crucial ever." When Ford proposed a potential Republican Party rival, Ronald Reagan, Kissinger dismissed him as "incompetent," agreeing with Ford that any Democrat would be a "disaster." On that same day Khmer Rouge soldiers, which had taken control of Cambodia the month before, hijacked the American cargo ship S.S. Mayaguez off the Cambodian coast, taking the crew prisoner and towing the ship to Koh Tang, about thirty miles off the Cambodian coast. When Kissinger got notice of the seizure, his reaction was indignant and belligerent: "We are not going to sit here and let an American merchant ship be captured at sea and let it go into the harbour without doing a bloody thing about it." At the NSC meeting later the same morning, Kissinger pushed hard for "a strong statement, a strong note and a show of force." He was joined in his campaign by his mentor, Vice President Rockefeller, who said, "If we do not respond violently we will get nibbled to death." President Ford, who feared a repeat of the

Pueblo episode, in which North Korea took a U.S. Navy intelligence ship, holding her crew hostage for almost a year, was resolved to act immediately. Kissin- ger's one worry was that launching military action from U.S. bases in Thailand would provoke a crisis with the Thai government and lead to the swift closure of those bases. But he was adamant that the United States must act, telling Ford, "At some point … the United States must draw the line … we must act upon it now, and act firmly."

SUMMER 1975: THE MIDDLE EAST, SOLZHENITSYN, AND THE HELSINKI ACCORDS

Gerald Ford's standing in the country rose as a result of the Mayaguez event, with reports putting him ahead of both his Democratic competitors and his potential Republican opponent, California's former governor Ronald Reagan. Because of his political clout, Kissinger persuaded Ford to take a strong stance against Israel during the "reassessment" of Middle East policy. Kissinger privately communicated his displeasure with the Israelis to President Ford and his deputy Scowcroft, telling Ford that their actions were an "outrage" and "an indignity to the United States." He desired "psychological warfare against Israel," claiming that their failure to negotiate an agreement with Egypt "blew up 18 months of US diplomacy." In a revealing remark, he lamented bitterly that it was "damn humiliating" that the Israelis seemed to believe "that I and the President needed this agreement ourselves." And the United States sorely needed a win." Kissinger frequently returned to the issue's domestic politics and his own personal participation. "I could keep the Middle East quiet through the '76 election," Ford was quoted as saying. "I did the same thing in '72 when Israel did the same thing to Rogers in '71," he says, referring to his self-serving and selective recall of those events.

If Kissinger assumed that being America's first Jewish secretary of state would provide him political cover to be harder on Israel, he was swiftly proven wrong. On May 22, 1975, shortly before Ford was to travel to Europe to meet with Sadat to discuss resuming negotiations, Senator Jacob Javits and seventy-five other senators urged the president to recognise that "preserving the peace requires that Israel obtain a level of military and economic support adequate to deter a renewal of war by Israel's neighbours." The letter advised Ford against suspending military aid to Israel and stated that America's national interests were "firmly with Israel in the search for peace in future negotiations, and that this premise is the basis of the current reassessment of U.S. policy in the Middle East." Kissinger felt that the Israeli embassy, particularly Ambassador Simcha Dinitz, was engaged in the letter's organisation. He explained to Ford that it demonstrated "Rabin's willingness to treat us as an antagonist." Kissinger also recognised that the Israelis had discovered the American position's Achilles' heel, with Congress essentially exerting itself in foreign policy across the board against an unelected president. Kissinger believed that Sadat would interpret the letter as an indication that America would be unable to persuade Israel to make any further concessions, causing the Egyptian leader to abandon his newfound admiration for America.

Kissinger became more confident about an interim accord after considering Sadat's suggested compromises. First, he had to persuade Prime Minister Rabin. Kissinger told Ford that Israeli Prime Minister Binyamin Netanyahu and his crew were the "world's worst shits," participating in a "pattern of deception" that made dealing with them a vexing experience. Kissinger sent precise instructions to Ford before the president's meeting with Rabin, urging him to be coldly accurate to the Israeli leader and to threaten Rabin with a return to the Geneva Conference and negotiations based on Israel's 1967 borders. The meeting between the two leaders was a disaster, with Ford believing there was "no give at all" in the Israeli stance and Kissinger believing they were simply "reselling their March proposal" and not moving any closer to compromise. When

Kissinger addressed Rabin about what the Israeli leader claimed was a "misunderstanding" concerning drawings of the Sinai they had provided, maps that appeared to indicate Israel would withdraw from the two passes, Kissinger's rage was obvious. "You must ask why Joe [Sisco], Brent Scowcroft, and I all have such a substantial misunderstanding," Kissinger said to Rabin, his voice dripping with disdain. You are correct. We never had disagreements with the Israeli government." However, the Israelis remained steadfast, prompting Kissinger to press Ford hard, telling him, "The tougher you are, the more chance there is to move them." Despite Ford's bleak outlook, Kissinger informed him, "I think they will cave." Ford issued a scathing ultimatum to the Israeli government at the end of June, calling the latest Israeli proposals "inadequate" and "counter to the interests of the United States and the world." According to Ford, this debate "went to the very heart of American-Israeli relations." Kissinger made certain that the "American ultimatum" became the headline story on network news. The Israelis were shaken, and Ambassador Dinitz flew to the Virgin Islands, where Kissinger was on vacation, to reassure him that the Israeli government was making a "serious effort" to avoid a crisis with "the gravest consequences for Israel, the United States, and the world."

Kissinger understood that Rabin's obstinacy stemmed from his weak domestic position, and that American pressure may assist him overcome cabinet opposition to the temporary arrangement. Indeed, Rabin told his cabinet that American pressure was as intense as that placed by the Eisenhower administration following the 1956 Suez crisis. Negotiations are currently moving forward, with the US promising both considerable economic and military aid to both countries, as well as the presence of Americans as monitors. Although Kissinger was able to persuade Israel to compromise with Egypt, he was still walking a tightrope in attempting to hold together the various, and at times conflicting, strands of his foreign policy framework. As the Middle East talks stretched on into the summer of

1975, Kissinger explained the politics of his strategy to Ford: "The reason I reluctantly came to an interim agreement is that if you get it, plus a SALT agreement and one or two others, you'll be in good shape in foreign policy." Kissinger was determined to maintain and strengthen détente with the Soviet Union, believing that the threat to Ford's 1976 election would come "if SALT blows up" and the Democrats went to the left to oppose the administration.

In retrospect, Kissinger's political judgement was not as bad as it appears. The future of relations with the Soviet Union seemed promising in July 1975. The Apollo-Soyuz space encounter took place on July 17, and it was extensively and positively covered by all three American television networks. Commentators frequently referred to the symbolism of the meeting in space, which would take place thirty years after the American-Soviet conference on the Elbe to end World War II, and predicted that it would one day represent the end of the Cold War.164 Ford's decision to attend the summit on Security and Cooperation in Europe (CSCE) in Helsinki, a summit that would ratify a set of agreements that the Soviets regarded a definitive settlement of World War II, went hand in hand with this public relations spectacular. Kissinger was not a fan of the CSCE, telling Ford, "We never wanted it, but we went along with the Europeans." To Kissinger, the entire affair was a "grandstand play to the Left," and many of the clauses for freedom of movement and information were "meaningless." Kissinger believed that the symbolism of the 35-nation conference, together with Ford's subsequent excursions to more independent-minded East European countries such as Romania and Yugoslavia, may assist in strengthening support for détente in the United States.

Kissinger's attempt to balance détente's cooperation and competition elements occasionally led to errors, none more damaging than the advice he gave to President Ford shortly before the CSCE to ignore Aleksandr Solzhenitsyn, the famous Russian writer and dissident who had been arrested and expelled from the Soviet Union in February 1974. The Russian writer was invited to the United States by Stanford University's Hoover Institution. Kissinger distinguished Solzhenitsyn's standing as an award-winning writer from his new role as a critic of the Soviet regime and an opponent of détente strategy. Kissinger believed that a meeting between Ford and Solzhenitsyn would further deteriorate US-Soviet relations, but he also resented how American opponents of détente were exploiting the heroic writer to criticise him and the Ford administration. Nonetheless, Ford's rejection of Solzhenitsyn highlighted schisms inside the government. Ford's youthful deputy assistant, Dick Cheney, stated that the US had shifted towards appeasing the Soviet system and had lost "faith in our fundamental principles concerning individual liberty and democracy." Cheney, on the other hand, maintained that détente "should consist of agreements wherever possible to reduce the possibility of conflict, but it does not mean that all of a sudden our relationship with the Soviets is all sweetness and light." Ford's refusal to meet with Solzhenitsyn became a campaign issue for both Democrats Scoop Jackson and Republicans Reagan. It also led to Ford's harsh public condemnation when he did go to Helsinki, which Solzhenitsyn referred to as the "funeral of Eastern Europe." The New York Times and The Wall Street Journal, whose editorial pages rarely agreed, both condemned the president for attending the summit and signing the Helsinki Accords, which they saw as legitimising Soviet rule over Eastern Europe.

Kissinger sounded conciliatory on human rights, even acknowledging the work of Minnesota Representative Donald Fraser, whose congressional hearings, along with those of Idaho Senator Frank Church and New York Representative Otis Pike, had regularly challenged Kissinger's actions. He said that the US does not "and will not condone repressive practices" and will "use our influence to oppose repressive practices." Our traditions and interests require it." Kissinger, on the other hand, tried to warn his liberal critics. "Truth compels also a recognition of our limits," he intoned, clearly indicating that he did not believe his audience recognised those limits. Kissinger considered it as a methodological issue: "The question is whether we promote human rights more effectively by counsel and friendly relations, where this serves our interest, or by confrontational propaganda and discriminatory legislation." Kissinger stated emphatically, "Our alliances and political relationships... are not favours to other governments, but reflect a recognition of mutual interests." They should be withdrawn only when our interests shift, not as punishment for any action with which we disagree." He also took aim at liberals who wanted the US to push more on human rights in South Korea and Indonesia while withdrawing from Vietnam. He went on to say, "It is the process of American disengagement that has eroded the sense of security and created a perceived need for greater internal discipline, and at the same time diminished our ability to influence domestic practices." As self-serving as that defence was, Kissinger was more honest and true when he added, "Painful experience should have taught us that we ought not exaggerate our capacity to foresee, let alone shape, social and political change in other societies." He continued by restating his views on how the United States should handle foreign policy: "The question is not whether our values should affect our foreign policy, but how." The question is whether we have the fortitude to face complexity and the inner resolve to deal with ambiguity; whether we will look past simple slogans and recognise that our great aims can only be achieved with patience and in imperfect phases."

The Heartland Speeches were a powerful and persuasive defence of Kissinger's foreign policy stance. However, Kissinger's ideas on human rights were far harsher than Winston Lord's pleasant words portrayed. Kissinger's inability to negotiate with congressional opponents on human rights issues, in fact, "stirred a hornet's nest." His opposition to even minor reform legislation backfired and "played a pivotal role in moving human rights from the sidelines to the centre of American diplomacy." Congressman James Abourezk later confessed that "dislike of Kissinger" was enough to get votes for human rights legislation. Kissinger's personalization of "his" foreign policy, as well as his insistence on maintaining tight control over it, backfired. He regarded legislative opposition as an attack on him personally, rather than a rejection of the idea. Although there was academic substance in his perspective of how best to advance American principles and human rights, Kissinger's approach against his congressional opponents ultimately backfired.

Domestic political reasons also played a role in Kissinger's ambition to nail down the Sinai II Agreement and salvage his failure from earlier in the year. In this situation, a combination of Sadat's idea of American specialists staffing the monitoring stations, together with a significant boost in military aid to Israel, helped generate a breakthrough in the talks. Kissinger reminded President Ford that his Democratic adversary, Scoop Jackson, had earlier ordered the Israeli envoy "not to make an interim agreement because it would only help you and me," and Kissinger evidently relished hurting Jackson by achieving an agreement. Kissinger also despised the degree to which the Israeli government informed its own people it was under significant American pressure to make concessions, or as he angrily told his assistant Joe Sisco, the Israelis are "putting out the word that they're being raped by us." When Kissinger eventually arrived in Israel in late August, he was confronted with "unprecedented hostility, mainly from right-wing opposition parties, and demonstrators accosted him at each stop." Although he achieved success with the Israelis on their withdrawal from the Mitla and Giddi passes, as well as relinquishing the Abu Rudeis and Ras Sudr oil fields, the magnitude of concessions and American obligations he was compelled to make to Israel infuriated Kissinger. He informed Ford that his meetings with the Israelis had "taken on more the character of exchanges between adversaries than between friends," and described the Israelis as "treacherous, petty, and deceitful."

The Sinai II agreement was reached on September 1, 1975, and was a crucial step toward the peace in the region, although the Ford administration made the same mistake it had with the Vladivostok summit and went beyond in portraying the deal to the public. Ford's staff arranged a televised transmission of the phone call between Ford and Kissinger—transparently designed "to establish the President's primacy over Kissinger in foreign affairs," with the result that Ford hyperbolically described the agreement as "the most historic, certainly, of this decade and perhaps in this century." White House reporters broke into "unkind but justified laughter" as Ford attempted to promise Anwar Sadat over a failing telephone connection that "we're going to keep the momentum going" for more accords. In dramatic contrast to the media adulation that greeted the Syrian disengagement agreement, NBC's Richard Valeriani simply commented that the arrangement was "modest good news" and concluded that it was the "best agreement that money could buy." That negative tone continued in the television coverage, with reporting on the Senate leader Mike Mansfield's concerns that American technicians in the Sinai could be the first step to "another Vietnam," and on Henry Jackson's insistence that Kissinger should swear "an oath" that there were no secret agreements in the settlement. Kissinger highlighted in congressional testimony that the presence of Americans in the Sinai was a "reluctant" concession to the Israelis and Egyptians, and that their "peacekeeping" function was not analogous to their involvement in Vietnam. Even the coverage of the actual signing in Geneva, with neither the Israelis nor the Egyptians acknowledging each other with words or a handshake, seemed to underscore the relative fragility of the peace, despite the administration's commitment of more than $2 billion in assistance to both Israel and Egypt.

CHALLENGES MOUNT: THE HALLOWEEN MASSACRE,

ANGOLA, AND THE DEMISE OF SALT

The subdued popular reaction to Sinai II served as a hint that foreign policy victory had lost part of its allure among an increasingly disillusioned American populace. Kissinger raged at Ford, claiming that despite the Sinai accord being "the greatest achievement since the opening to China," Congress "was pissing all over it." The most serious source of Kissinger's annoyance was not Sinai II, which Congress eventually approved, but the ongoing challenges to his position and policies. The congressional inquiries, particularly those of the House Intelligence Committee, sought to call as witnesses State Department personnel who had disagreed with Kissinger's Cyprus strategy, such as Thomas Boyatt. Kissinger's refusal to allow this resulted in a public brawl and a contempt citation, though Kissinger held his own in television news coverage of the committee's sessions. This challenge was accompanied by a confrontation with Defense Secretary Schlesinger over détente and the chance of a SALT II agreement. A Department of Defense intelligence report was leaked to The New York Times in early October. The pamphlet was harshly critical of détente, stating that "the Soviet Union is using détente policy to gain dominance over the West in all fields." The report stated, in a clear reference to a prospective SALT II accord, that "Soviet détente policy has facilitated Soviet strategic nuclear expansion and the cancelling out of US superiority, without provoking extensive Western country efforts." According to ABC's Barrie Dunsmore, conservative organisations backing Ronald Reagan were distributing copies of the report. He went on to warn Ford, "Schlesinger is making it tough for you with the Reagan bunch, but if you move to the right the liberals will kill you in the election for sabotaging détente." Ford agreed, but told Kissinger that he intended to give Schlesinger another chance, saying, "I want a SALT agreement." I want to process my conversation with [Schlesinger] before speaking with him again next week." Kissinger offered the president some talking points on what "should be coming from the Pentagon" to back a pro-SALT stance, adding a comment that was plainly intended to drive Ford into action: "Haig says he [Schlesinger] wants to be President."

Kissinger then left for China to complete the preparations for Ford's trip to Beijing. Ford wanted Kissinger to assist him politically without appearing to be a carbon copy of Nixon, and he insisted on doing "something different" from what Nixon had done on his trip, but "dramatic" enough to garner substantial television coverage. Kissinger recommended visiting Xi'an, the ancient Chinese capital, and advised Ford that a communiqué that reaffirmed the Shanghai Communiqué of 1972 would be better for Ford domestically. Unfortunately for Kissinger, he ran into a Chinese leadership keen on lecturing him even more vehemently about the dangers of détente. Deng Xiaoping, now vice premier and successor to Zhou Enlai, even compared détente to Chamberlain's appeasement policy prior to World War II. To Kissinger's chagrin, the Chinese constantly emphasised American weakness. Kissinger attempted to spin the news by telling reporters that the Chinese would enjoy seeing Americans and Russians "at each other's throats." The coverage of Kissinger's visit, on the other hand, focused on the Chinese critique of détente and the lack of progress in US-China ties. It was an apt foreshadowing of what awaited Kissinger when he returned to the United States.

On Saturday, October 25, Kissinger came into the Oval Office to report on his China trip to President Ford, informing him that the relationship had "cooled" substantially and that "Mao's theme is our weakness." Unaware of Ford's personnel preparations, Kissinger stated that Mao told him that "he likes Schlesinger's view of the Soviet Union better than mine" and that he wanted the defence secretary to visit China to "drive the Soviet Union wild." Later that afternoon, Ford summoned Kissinger and Donald Rumsfeld to inform them that he had decided to fire Schlesinger and install Rumsfeld as defence secretary, while delegating Kissinger's duties as national security adviser to Kissinger's deputy, Brent Scowcroft. Kissinger attempted to persuade the president that he would be blamed for the firing and that losing his post as national security adviser would harm his reputation in foreign capitals. But Ford was adamant about the shake-up, expecting it would restore his administration's sense of leadership. He was caught off guard by the unfavourable feedback. NBC Nightly News sought a response from Henry Jackson, who attacked the administration's "one-man operation" in foreign policy, presenting Schlesinger's removal as a victory for Kissinger. If the sacking of Schlesinger signalled Kissinger's power, Ford's withdrawal of Vice President Rockefeller from consideration as his running mate signalled Ford's willingness to please conservative Republicans.

Kissinger agreed with the Washington consensus that the measures were being orchestrated by Donald Rumsfeld in order to boost his own position within the Ford administration. Kissinger stated in his first press conference following the shake-up that his relationship with the president was "excellent" and "unchanged." Kissinger praised Schlesinger, calling him "a man of outstanding ability and one of the best analysts of defence matters." Kissinger's nearly "lyrical" praise for Schlesinger was compared with Kissinger's brusque comment on Rumsfeld, adding that "heartfelt praise does not spring readily" from Kissinger when speaking of Rumsfeld. Kissinger paused and haltingly responded to a reporter's question on Rumsfeld's qualifications for defence secretary, finally remarking that Rumsfeld is "a man who is very attuned to the political process," a stinging praise. When asked if he would "last out" President Ford's term, Kissinger joked that he no longer answered his phone on Sundays, a not-so-subtle criticism of how the firings were handled, and allowed Koppel to observe that the Ford administration's "internal bickering" was not over. Kissinger likewise avoided answering directly whether he had threatened to resign. Kissinger did, in fact, undergo a brief depression, similar to what he had experienced when Nixon made him the scapegoat for his disastrous South Asian policy. He gathered a group of friends, including Winston and Bette Lord, Lawrence Eagleburger, William Simon, and David Bruce, in need of both reassurance and pity. The London Times correspondent Henry Brandon commented that the dinner party felt "like a gathering of the last loyalists." They discussed drafts of a resignation letter, which included goals that Kissinger still hoped the administration would fulfil. Finally, Kissinger agreed to see the president, but Ford talked him out of it. In his autobiography, Ford stated, "The country needed him—I needed him—to implement our foreign policy at this difficult time."

Kissinger continued to advocate for détente and another SALT accord. He collaborated with Time's White House correspondent Hugh Sidey on an extremely sympathetic article in which Kissinger was portrayed as trying to keep the country from reverting "back to the days of the cold war and bitter confrontation with the Soviet Union" by preserving "the new relationship" of détente. Kissinger was "simply brighter and more adept at the art of human persuasion than any of his adversaries," according to Sidey, and Kissinger's reading of American politics, specifically those Americans "in the farm areas [who] want Russian markets for their grain," might allow him to pull off "a miracle or two." Kissinger emphasised in a November 24 speech in Detroit commemorating the last six years of foreign policy achievements that "foreign policy must be based on reality, not rhetoric," and that "today's reality is that we live in a world of nuclear equality." Kissinger said that instead of "constant crises" with the Soviet Union, there were now talks on a variety of themes, including arms control, economic cooperation, and international affairs. Although he admitted that détente had been overstated, he argued that the task for Americans was to "manage a fundamental conflict of values in the shadow of nuclear holocaust."

As they prepared to go for China in late November, Kissinger was certain that they could replicate Nixon's election-year success. Brezhnev's offer to Kissinger to meet with him when they returned from China was a good sign. Kissinger even predicted that he may reactivate the "Soviet-Chinese triangle." Following their arrival in China, Kissinger attempted to persuade the Chinese that he shared their concerns about the Soviets, but added, "We are promoting the strongest policy against the Soviet Union that we can before the elections." He attempted to persuade the Chinese to help him characterise US-China relations as excellent and improving, claiming that "our opponents will use any issue to undermine the credibility of what we are doing." The Chinese did limit the amount of news that came out of the sessions, and Kissinger delivered the press briefing at the end of Ford's visit, portraying the negotiations in the best light possible while leaving American reporters with the simple remark, "We are satisfied with the visit." This strategy was mostly successful. Kissinger's statement that not much time was spent on détente was reported on all three network newscasts, and on NBC, Tom Brokaw even observed that Kissinger was successful in getting the Chinese to tone down their "bombastic rhetoric" about détente.

When Kissinger returned to Washington, it was not Portuguese East Timor that he was required to address. Angola, a Portuguese colony, obtained independence on November 11, 1975, and was quickly engulfed in civil strife. Earlier in the year, Kissinger was instrumental in convincing Ford to authorise covert American financial support for the National Front for the Liberation of Angola (FNLA), led by Holden Roberto, a close ally of Zaire's leader, Mobutu Sese Seko—a group that had also received Chinese assistance. This American money empowered the FNLA to launch an offensive, motivating other factions to seek outside assistance. The Popular Movement for the Liberation of Angola (MPLA) held sway in the capital city of Luanda and had gained support from the Soviet Union and Cuba. China and South Africa backed the National Union for Total Independence of Angola (UNITA) in the south. Throughout 1975, the US and the Soviet Union increasingly boosted their assistance for its friends, with the US now also assisting UNITA and the FNLA. According to Kissinger, "If all the surrounding countries see Angola go communist, they will assume the United States has no will." The United States sent $14 million in July and an additional $10.7 million in early September.

Kissinger faced strong opposition within the State Department from the chief of the Africa Bureau, Nathaniel Davis, who argued that the United States' fundamental interests were not at stake and that the risks of interference outweighed the potential advantages. Davis also stated that the CIA's tactics in Angola were "inadequate to achieve the outlined goals." Davis echoed Kissinger's concerns about the Angolan operation's internal politics, suggesting that if they couldn't muster the political will to make a substantial effort, it would be far better to do nothing at all. After his objections to the Angolan incursion were overruled, Davis departed, and Kissinger protested to Ford that the African Bureau would disclose its objections to the press. Ford, persuaded by Kissinger, claimed that if the US did nothing, "we will lose Southern Africa," adding, "I won't let someone in Foggy Bottom deter me."

Kissinger was enraged by the Cuban participation, claiming that they were acting as Soviet surrogates, "paying back the Soviets for their military and economic support." Kissinger referred to Castro as a "pipsqueak," believing the Cuban leader was "thumbing his nose" at the US. The potential impact of Angola on détente and his efforts to get a SALT deal was far more significant to Kissinger than reconciliation with Cuba. When the scope of the Cuban help became clear in November 1975, Kissinger urged the CIA to enhance covert aid significantly to match the Soviet-Cuban effort. He also issued a severe public warning to the Soviets, declaring that they were violating the 1972 pact on "Principles of Co-existence" and urged a

"African solution to an African problem." At the same time, he wanted to create a legitimate way out of the problem for the Soviets. He told NBC's Richard Valeriani that he believed their action was motivated by competitiveness with the Chinese and that they had no intention of challenging the US. He said that Ford could not appear "soft" against the Russians, expecting that the politburo would take Ford's internal political problems into account.

Along with his public efforts, Kissinger wrote a confidential note to the Soviets in which he decried the "efforts [the Soviet Union] is now making to escalate the fighting in Angola," arguing that if they continued, they would "set back the progress of détente." Kissinger's note exaggerated the facts when it stated, "The United States for its part pursues no unilateral interests in Angola and is exclusively concerned with seeing the people of that country live in peace, independence, and well-being." As deceptive as such claims were, they did reveal Kissinger's wish that Angola would not become a battleground for the Russians. Unfortunately for Kissinger, the Soviets found themselves in a winning scenario in Angola, winning on the ground with their Cuban friends and in the court of African opinion by opposing South Africa's apartheid system. They defended their endorsement of the MPLA as Angola's legitimate government and matched the Americans in deception, declaring that "not a single Soviet man is taking part in the hostilities in Angola." Kissinger and Ford summoned the Soviet ambassador, Dobrynin, and begged him for assistance with his superiors in Moscow. Kissinger informed the Russian, "We can't defend our people against your massive airlift and Cuban troops." Ford went on to say, "I am for détente but this is difficult for me to explain."

The idea that a $60 million clandestine attempt to support rebel forces in Angola could remain secret during a year in which both the Senate and House were examining the intelligence community is preposterous. Seymour Hersh detailed the entire scope of the Angola program in a New York Times report on December 13, 1975. Senate Democrats, backed by Richard Clark, have launched a campaign to limit funding for Angola. The media, particularly CBS Evening News, drew comparisons between Angola's engagement and the start of the Vietnam War. Walter Cronkite was explicit about the connection in a five-day series of reports, arguing "that America became so heavily involved in Vietnam because the government did not share enough of its decisions with the people," and that the purpose of this reporting was "to try to play our small part in preventing that mistake this time." Senators repeatedly brought up the Vietnam analogy during the Clark Amendment debate, which cut off financing for Angolan operations and was approved by the Senate by a vote of 54 to 22.

Kissinger fought aggressively against the congressional proposals, but he was unable to alter public opinion. "We are living in a nihilistic nightmare," he warned Ford, referring to SALT critics who complained about the Soviets having too many SS-19 missiles but then "caved" in Angola. Kissinger's rage overlooks the extent to which his policies energised adversaries on both the right and left sides of the political spectrum. Overselling détente aided the right in portraying the ongoing rivalry with the Soviets as a one-way path. The left was driven by the prospect of competing with the Soviet Union in a Third World country with minimal strategic relevance. Kissinger's path between these two schools of criticism was complicated by his personalization of all foreign policy issues, as well as his tendency for secrecy and dishonesty. Despite his flaws, Kissinger was correct about the dilemma confronting American foreign policy. Kissinger informed Ford that America's goal was to "manage the emergence of the Soviets to superpower status without a war." He was concerned that Congress was depriving the president of "both carrot and stick," and, echoing his previous condemnation of "massive retaliation" two decades before, he informed Ford, "We will soon be in the position of nuclear war or nothing."

Even though Kissinger was furious about Angola, he still believed he could reach an agreement with the Russians on SALT. He rescheduled his travel to Moscow from December to January to allow more time for the American stance to be determined, particularly to gain the support of the Defense Department. Kissinger viewed SALT through the lens of détente and domestic politics. "We have the SALT agreement within our grasp," Kissinger informed Ford, referring to Henry Jackson, who was still regarded as Ford's most likely Democratic opponent. We can annihilate our opponents." He urged the president for some wiggle room in negotiating the range of various cruise missiles, both air and sea-launched, as well as wiggle room in dealing with the Soviets over their Backfire bomber. Kissinger felt that Rumsfeld's Defense Department was reverting to a "stonewall position," and encouraged Ford to inform Rumsfeld that "you are determined to get an agreement and you want them to get with it." Ford responded, "I want something very forthcoming because I happen to agree it is good substantively and good politically."

Gerald Ford needed to be "good politically" in January 1976. In mid-December, his approval rating had dropped to 39%. The Senate setback over Angola exacerbated the damage, but Ford remained committed to Kissinger and détente. When asked about American foreign policy on a special NBC program, Ford argued, "If the American people take a good, calculated look at the benefits of détente, I think they will support it rather than oppose it." And, politically, I believe that any politician who says we should forsake détente would lose in the long term." Kissinger took a slightly different strategy, attempting to prioritise détente and his efforts to get a SALT agreement over party concerns. He emphasised that "partisan controversy" would be a "tragedy" if it interfered with his negotiations in Moscow. He also stressed that any SALT deal would not be "a concession we make to the Soviet Union, but it is an objective that is in our own interest." Despite admitting that the

Angola problem was harming relations, Kissinger claimed that SALT II was so crucial that it "bridges differences" between the superpowers. He urged his media contacts to cover the possibility of a deal and to remind Americans of the necessity of détente. In a New York Times essay, Reston argued that even a "limited compromise" on SALT II would be "a political event in the [1976 presidential election] campaign." Such a move would "help the President ease the pressure on détente, and the Russians, and this may have been what Moscow had in mind by inviting Mr. Kissinger to the Soviet Union in the first place." On the day of Kissinger's journey to Moscow, ABC's Ted Koppel launched a three-part series on détente, emphasising Kissinger's perspective on its importance in lessening the threat of nuclear war and emphasising the ways it benefitted America's interests.

Kissinger exaggerated when he told Anatoly Dobrynin that coming to Moscow was "political suicide," but his negotiating position was the weakest since he took office. He was presenting two conflicting offers from a divided American administration, with an unelected president under political siege, attempting to sway the Soviets on an issue, Angola, where they held all the cards. The talks got off to a shaky start when a reporter yelled whether Angola will be covered, to which Brezhnev answered, "I have no questions about Angola." Angola is not my homeland." Kissinger interrupted that it would be discussed, but Brezhnev disregarded this brutally. In private, Kissinger continued to emphasise the issue, saying it was "intolerable" that Cuba had launched an "invasion" and that the superpowers "must exercise restraint." Brezhnev insisted, "Are we here to discuss SALT? Or maybe Angola?" He stated unequivocally, "There is no Soviet military presence in Angola." At the end of the discussion, Brezhnev said, "We hope we can reach an agreement and that it will help Ford's situation." Kissinger welcomed that remark, but continued, "I agree you have nothing to gain in Angola." In Angola, we have nothing to gain. But there are 8000 Cubans running around..."

Despite his displeasure with the Soviet leader's handling of Angola, Kissinger believed that the SALT discussions had been successful and that a solution was feasible. The Soviets remained certain that their Backfire bomber was not a long-range bomber and so should not be counted under the agreement. Brezhnev even dispatched a Soviet commander to give the Americans a detailed breakdown of the bomber's capabilities. Moscow showed some adaptability in coping with the many types of American cruise missiles. A second deal linking the Soviet deployment of Backfire bombers with the US right to deploy cruise missiles on twenty-five surface ships and a readiness to forgo longer-range cruise missiles on submarines could be one conceivable compromise. Brezhnev appeared favourable, and Kissinger and his staff believed they had made a breakthrough.

Kissinger claimed the Defense Department was "stonewalling" and encouraged the president to reconvene the National Security Council "and lay down the law." Ford, on the other hand, was hesitant to confront Rumsfeld and the Pentagon, and sought a compromise solution once more. Despite his continuing promotion of the significance of a SALT treaty, Kissinger knew that "he could no longer force the pace on SALT without building up an insurmountable opposition that would rebound against Ford in the election campaign." Furthermore, the Defense Department's opposition was ultimately rooted in many in James Schlesinger's former domain's suspicion that Kissinger and Ford wanted SALT for primarily political and personal reasons, and that Kissinger, in particular, was willing to play fast and loose with technical issues in order to reach an agreement. Rumsfeld, in particular, claimed that the Soviets were breaking the first SALT accord by concealing missile silos and other military facilities. More importantly, he wished to postpone any pact "that required restricting our cruise missile technologies as part of the deal." To appease his critics, Kissinger agreed to the Pentagon's compromise plan to set aside the Backfire and cruise missile difficulties in order to complete a treaty on other subjects. When this was conveyed to the Soviets, Brezhnev warned Ford it was a "step backward," and Ford believed that a SALT treaty before the election was probably unattainable.

Kissinger remained committed to assisting Ford's reelection. He warned Ford that he was concerned about America's position in the world following the Angola disaster, which was "reopening the Vietnam wounds." Kissinger remained convinced that "we have a damned good foreign policy" and that the administration should go on the offensive in proclaiming it. Possibly recalling his experience with Nixon during the 1972 campaign, he reminded the president, "We have got to show you are a winner." Kissinger privately harboured reservations about Ford and was not always shy about expressing them. He remarked to British pals, "I seem destined to work for losers." Kissinger sharply chastised Ford on Angola during an off-the-record discussion with the Boston Globe's editorial board, stating that he should have followed Nixon's lead and bypassed Congress. Fortunately for Kissinger, the criticism was never published.

KISSINGER'S LAST CAMPAIGN: RONALD REAGAN, AFRICA, AND THE 1976 ELECTION

The British ambassador in Washington, Peter Ramsbotham, disagreed with Berlin's description of "gloom and self-contempt" in the United States in an April 1976 letter to his friend Isaiah Berlin, but added, "Henry Kissinger has a split personality in Washington—or at least he enjoys the pretence of it." Kissinger, according to Ramsbotham, frequently indulged the "Spenglerian side of his nature—as a historian, he probably believes that the democratic pattern in the West, created by the British and Americans, cannot be sustained indefinitely." The U.S. ambassador stated, "In his role as Secretary of State, he is actively searching for new initiatives to assert the power of the United States in the world." Ramsbotham questioned if another secretary of state had ever been "so optimistically intent on trying to manipulate power in the national interest."

Ramsbothams insight encapsulated the basic conflict between the intellectual and political Kissinger. In private, Kissinger was pessimistic about America's political climate and his own personal predicament. Kissinger's pessimism, particularly his speculations on America's collapse, became "the only red-hot issue" in the Republican primary race. Despite his concerns about his job security and legacy, Kissinger remained active. As Ramsbotham pointed out, he actively sought new places to apply the Kissinger magic, both to assert American strength and, as he had learned from Nixon in 1972, to assist Ford in remaining president. Kissinger also vehemently defended his foreign policy and slammed his detractors while being a consistent presence in the media. Despite the fact that some of Ford's staff wanted him to leave, the president's personal backing remained strong, and Kissinger desired four more years on the job.

External events helped Kissinger. Left-wing militants assassinated CIA station head Richard Welch in Greece on December 23, 1975. Although his assassination was unrelated to the congressional investigations, it enabled the Ford administration to respond to the House Intelligence Committee's accusations on the CIA. The whole House opted in late January not to release the Pike Committee's report. When the study was leaked to The Village Voice, which publicised charges against Kissinger, he used a press conference to call it a "new version of McCarthyism." When a reporter inquired if Kissinger would retire, he demonstrated the same dramatic ability he had displayed eighteen months previously in Salzburg. He said he would be willing to relinquish his position if it "was in the interest of American foreign policy," then proceeded to ask "whether the style of public debate should be that any public figure can be destroyed by the most irresponsible and flagrant charges and that then the argument should be made that the effectiveness is affected because totally irresponsible and essentially untrue charges are made." His vehement denial was the lead story on all three television networks that evening, coupled with a claim that President Ford told New Hampshire reporters that he wanted Kissinger to be his secretary of state for the next term. Richard Nixon contacted Kissinger to express his admiration for his "honest emotional outrage" and to tell him, "I thought your press conference was splendid." It had favourable coverage in the press, which is unimportant, but it performed exceptionally well on television."

Although Kissinger hoped that Nixon's visit to China would be beneficial to the government, Ford and his political aides were concerned about public opinion. Ford's tight victory over Reagan in the New Hampshire primary on February 24 came as a shock. Nonetheless, Ford blamed Nixon's travel to China for the tight result, claiming that it reminded Americans of Watergate and his contentious pardon. "What possessed the President to pop off again?" exclaimed Kissinger to Scowcroft. He went on to argue that it "makes him look weak to say Nixon can hurt him." After attacking Ford's political aides, Kissinger warned Scowcroft that Ford was making a mistake by not "claiming a success in foreign policy," and he lamented, "If he does not get out ahead soon in foreign policy, I will be destroyed." Scowcroft pledged to deliver the message, but Ford had other ideas. In an interview with a Florida newspaper, Ford slammed the "timing" of Nixon's trip to China once more. He then dropped a bombshell by declaring that he would no longer use the word "détente" and would instead speak of "peace through strength." Despite the president's continuous defence of Kissinger, Ford was plainly reacting to popular opinion. In reporting Ford's decision, NBC observed that, according to its most recent poll, 64 percent of Americans believed the Soviet Union benefited more from détente than the United States.

Kissinger was displeased by Ford's decision, voicing his displeasure privately while also displaying his sense of humour in public. Senator Abraham Ribicoff of Connecticut chastised Kissinger for not joining the Soviet Union in pressuring France and Germany to limit their export of nuclear fuel to other countries during Senate proceedings a week after Ford's interview. Ribicoff yelled angrily that if Americans couldn't work cooperatively with the Soviets, "we should toss the whole concept of détente into the sewer." "Well, Senator, there's great activity in that direction as it is," Kissinger answered, and the audience began to chuckle. Kissinger later justified "the forbidden word" as vital in a world where superpowers may annihilate each other. Kissinger continued, "There is no consistent standard for criticising détente." Some accused the Ford administration for being too mild on the Soviet Union, while others argued that the US did not work effectively with the Soviet Union against its old allies. Kissinger's juxtaposition of these attacks on détente was intended to show the administration's middle ground and, by extension, the policy's soundness.

Then there was the primary in North Carolina. Reagan began hammering the government over the Panama Canal and the discussions Kissinger was then conducting to return the canal to Panama in the late stages of the Florida campaign. Although the issue did not turn the tide in Florida for Reagan, it did provide him with an emotionally resonant applause line: "It's ours! We made it! We had to pay for it! And it's something we should keep!" The Panama Canal issue acted as a sort of compensation for the humiliation of failure in Vietnam for many Americans. In North Carolina, Reagan emphasised the issue, which helped propel him to a surprise victory. Reagan's attacks on the Panama Canal, Kissinger, and détente were lauded by all three networks. While reporting a Ford event in California, NBC Nightly News correspondent John Cochran stated that "a lot of Republicans just don't like Henry Kissinger," but Ford's commitment to Kissinger remained. Reagan escalated the onslaught by purchasing a half-hour of NBC airtime on March 31. The former California governor began his address by discussing the economy and government expenditure, but the sections that made headlines were on foreign policy. Reagan used a passage from former Admiral Elmo Zumwalt's soon-to-be-published memoir to reiterate his anti-disarmament stance. Reagan said that Kissinger informed Zumwalt, "The day of the United States has passed, and today is the day of the Soviet Union," and that "my job as Secretary of State is to negotiate the most acceptable second-best position available." Reagan maintained the spotlight on Kissinger, noting that Kissinger's assistant, Helmut Sonnenfeldt, whom Reagan referred to as "[Kissinger's] Kissinger," had expressed "the belief that, in effect, the captive nations should give up any claim of national sovereignty and simply become part of the Soviet Union," or, as Reagan put it, "slaves should accept their fate." Reagan concluded his speech by declaring that he was not willing to send America to the "dustbin of history," saying, "We're Americans, and we have a rendezvous with destiny." More than $1.5 million was raised as a result of the speech.

Kissinger was well aware that Reagan had stumbled across a delicate subject. Kissinger had a disagreement with Secretary of Defense Donald Rumsfeld in front of President Ford two days before Reagan's address, telling Rumsfeld, "The impression that we are slipping is creating a bad impression around the world," to which Rumsfeld replied, "But it's true." Kissinger wrote to Reagan, saying, "I think the posture to take is that Reagan doesn't know what he's talking about and is irresponsible." Kissinger also desired a harder and more aggressive posture toward the Cubans. Kissinger had been warning the Cubans about possible American reprisal, including a blockade, if they intervened in Africa again. Kissinger's hard words, which some TV reporters regarded as "election year toughness," upset Rumsfeld. "I think we'll kill ourselves if we make threats and Congress passes a resolution prohibiting any action," the defence secretary warned Ford. Ford answered that he did not want "communists to get the idea that we would not take drastic action."

Kissinger received a brief political reprieve when Ford won the Wisconsin primary just over a week after Reagan's address. Ford opted to view his success as "fully justifying my faith in Henry Kissinger," and insisted that his staff back "one of the greatest secretaries of state in American history." Ford's insistence was necessary but ineffective. His campaign chair, Rogers Morton, announced that Kissinger would quit the administration, and in the run-up to the Texas primary at the end of the month, Ford workers speculated that John Connally would be Ford's candidate to replace him. Reporters also liked contrasting Ford's remarks about Kissinger to what he made about Nelson Rockefeller before dropping him off the ticket. When asked about Morton, Kissinger reacted violently, saying, "Is Morton running for President?" He used comedy more effectively. In response to how Deng Xiaoping's recent fall from popularity in China was communicated to the West, Kissinger expressed sympathy for the Chinese leader, adding, "I'm in the wall-poster stage myself."

Kissinger devised a strategy to avoid becoming a wall poster. Winston Lord had sent Kissinger a memo earlier in the year equating the current situation in southern Africa to what Kissinger faced in the Middle East in 1973. The document asserted that Kissinger had successfully realigned the situation and pushed the Soviets out of the Middle East, citing the Soviet alignment with "progressive" forces, the Arabs, and the American relationship to Israel. The similar possibility for American mediation now exists in Southern Africa. The British launched a new campaign in late March to try to bring about a peaceful settlement in Rhodesia. Ian Smith, the white head of the breakaway state, however, rejected it. Despite worldwide censure, Smith and his allies declared independence unilaterally in November 1965, enduring economic penalties and political isolation.

The fall of the Portuguese empire, the independence of Angola and Mozambique, and the growing Cuban presence in the region, however, radically altered the environment in which Rhodesia lived. Kissinger now considered the US to be "the only power capable of influencing the calculations of the parties." When the new CIA director, George H. W. Bush informed Kissinger that the Cubans would be fighting in Rhodesia by the end of the year, Kissinger realised he had to fly to Africa. "Basically, I am with the whites in Southern Africa," he said Ford, "but in my comments, I will support majority rule in Rhodesia." I'll say the same thing about South Africa, but in a gentler tone."

Kissinger applauded Ford for modifying his strategy toward southern Africa without considering domestic politics. But, as with détente, Kissinger was considering the general election. He recognized the administration's electoral benefit in adopting majority rule in southern Africa, countering the Democrats' moralistic attack on foreign policy. With the guerrilla fight against the Rhodesian government intensifying and an explosion of instability in South Africa's cities, warnings of a racial war looming were becoming more widespread, and an American effort to prevent it would attract votes. The prospect that Cubans may take an active part, backed by the Soviets, brought Cold War considerations into play, though Kissinger realised that America could never intervene militarily to assist racially discriminatory governments like Rhodesia's or South Africa's. Kissinger then made tremendous attempts to get domestic support for his proposals. This policy shift related to Ford's own sense of right and wrong, his inherent "decency," and his recognition that the American national interest would be better served by putting America squarely behind majority rule. However, political motivations were not lacking. "There are times when the politically expedient can be morally wise," Martin Luther King, Jr. once said. Aside from the moral problems at stake, Kissinger surely anticipated that a diplomatic victory in Africa would bring some gloss back to his own reputation.

Kissinger delivered one of his most important and moving speeches in April 1976 in Lusaka, Zambia's capital, affirming that America supported "self-determination, majority rule, equal rights, and human dignity for all the peoples of southern Africa—in the name of moral principle, international law, and world peace." "Our support for this principle [majority rule] in southern Africa is not simply a matter of foreign policy, but an imperative of our moral heritage," he continued, adding that the Rhodesia regime will face America's "unrelenting opposition until a negotiated settlement is achieved." It was an unusually optimistic address, prompting Zambian President Kenneth Kaunda to openly cry. Despite fears about how African leaders would react to him, Kissinger managed the trip expertly, earning praise not just from Kaunda, who was considered pro-Western, but also from Tanzania's more suspicious Julius Nyerere. Kissinger told Nyerere that Arab countries were distrustful before 1973, but now that "we're giving $1 billion to Egypt in aid and [Sadat] has reclaimed more territory than any other Arab leader," they are less so. He went on to say, "I like to think we can do the same with Africa on a cooperative basis, and work with you." Later, Nyerere told a British ambassador that Kissinger might be able to push through a majority rule agreement, and that "there may yet be a chance for the war in Rhodesia to be brought to an end more quickly than had previously seemed possible." Kissinger, avoiding the arrogance he'd displayed on previous occasions, told African leaders he was there to listen and learn, and maintained that "African problems should be solved by African solutions."

Despite the fact that Kissinger was hundreds of miles away, Ronald Reagan maintained his concentration on him. In response to the Lusaka speech, Reagan stated, "I'm afraid that we're going to have a massacre." He continued with a more serious tone: "We seem to be embarking on a policy of dictating to the people of southern Africa and running the risk of increased violence and bloodshed in an area already beset with tremendous antagonism and difficulties." Reagan's argument appealed to racial anger without addressing domestic issues such as busing, crime, or affirmative action, and it connected with George Wallace supporters in Texas, who could—and did— cross over to vote for Reagan. When Reagan won a landslide victory in Texas on May 1, Kissinger was blamed. In his New York Times piece, William Safire contended that Ford's defeat stemmed from underestimating Reagan and failing to fire Kissinger. Kissinger's visit had a "devastating effect" in the South, according to Robert Michel, the assistant House Republican leader, and he should be "muzzled." On NBC Nightly News, Senate Minority Whip Robert Griffin stated that one Republican political adviser at a leadership conference advised Ford that Kissinger "ought to go."

On May 7, Kissinger returned from Africa with only his wife and low-level State Department officials to greet him. Marvin Kalb made the key point that President Ford would have been present in the past. All things being equal, Kissinger told reporters that he would prefer not to continue on for another four years, a statement that left the door open for change if the president requested him to stay. At the same time, Kissinger marshalled a defence of his record and position, with great assistance from media friends. According to ABC's Ted Koppel, Ford's campaign is built on the "twin pillars" of a growing economy and a successful "imaginative" foreign policy. Kissinger was critical to international policy, particularly dealing with the Soviet Union and the Middle East, and firing him may cost the president support from moderate voters. In a positive assessment of the Africa tour, NBC's Richard Valeriani noted that, despite political issues, Kissinger remained "the most respected public figure in the country." Some of Kissinger's harshest detractors praised the shift in African policy. "However ignoble its immediate origins and motivation, the revised African policy that Gerald Ford authorised and Henry Kissinger enunciated is right," wrote John Osborne in The

New Republic. It is morally correct, and I believe it will be politically and strategically correct in the long run." By the end of the month, although trailing Reagan in the delegate count, Ford told the Los Angeles Press Club that he wanted Kissinger to remain as secretary of state in a Ford government.

Kissinger took a brief detour from his Africa activities in early June to attend an Organization of American States (OAS) summit in Chile. Despite the fact that the Church Committee report clearly stated that Nixon and Kissinger collaborated to topple the Allende regime, Kissinger utilised his trip to Santiago to try to bolster his new image in public. With his African diplomacy in the spotlight, Kissinger began speaking as an advocate of democracy in foreign policy and "referred to human rights in 40 percent of his speeches." He delivered a statement at the OAS summit in which he condemned Chile's administration for "violations of elemental international standards of human rights," and projected that unless Chile implemented reforms, relations with the US would suffer. Kissinger's outward support for human rights was not matched by a shift in his personal diplomacy with tyrants such as General Pinochet. "We are sympathetic with what you are trying to do here," he informed the Chilean leader privately. Kissinger stated that he had to deal with "massive domestic problems, in all branches of the government especially Congress, but also in the Executive, over the issue of human rights." Two days later, Kissinger made the same appeal to General Videla's new Argentine military government, which had taken power in a coup in March 1976. The regime imposed martial law, and the "Dirty War" would kill thousands of Argentines over the next several years, many of whom simply "disappeared." The United States, like Indonesia and Chile, was more concerned with protecting an anti-communist ally than with preserving human rights. "We are aware you are in a difficult period," Kissinger told Argentina's foreign minister, César Augusto Guzzetti. It is an odd period, when political, criminal, and terrorist operations seem to converge without distinction. We understand that you need to build power." Kissinger did try to persuade the Argentines to "return quickly to normal procedures" and stop focusing solely on terrorism. "We want you to succeed," Kissinger told Argentina's president. We don't want to bother you. I will do my best. Of course, you realise that means I'll be hounded. But I've observed that after a certain level of personal torture, you become invulnerable." Kissinger did promise Guzzetti that "no matter what happens," he would return to Argentina for the 1978 World Cup.

Following his return from South America, Kissinger planned a meeting with South African Prime Minister John Vorster at Bodenmais, a rural Bavarian village in Germany. Kissinger believed that South Africa held the key to regional growth. South African police opened fire on students protesting the use of Afrikaans in school on June 16, 1976. The incident sparked the worst rioting in South African history, with over a hundred people dead in the first ten days of protests. The United Nations denounced South Africa for the Soweto massacres, casting doubt on Kissinger's planned meeting with Vorster. Nonetheless, Kissinger went forward with it, possibly assuming that the domestic turmoil would make Vorster more willing to forsake Rhodesia and reduce South Africa's international isolation.

Kissinger approached Vorster with sympathy, recognizing that he was "a newcomer to Africa," but telling him that Rhodesia was "an unwinnable situation, no matter how long it takes, whether five or ten years." Kissinger anticipated defeat by comparing the situation to that of Algeria, where French colonists had really been there longer than whites had been in Rhodesia. He gave Vorster two options: try to promote majority rule in Rhodesia or play for time while the situation deteriorated. Kissinger said it was "as fundamental a decision as any South African prime minister had ever faced." Kissinger also stated emphatically that the United States could do little to assist Smith's Rhodesia, citing America's own racial politics. "With fifty percent of our combat troops being black because of our all-volunteer Army," the truth was that there was no "domestic situation in which we could support Smith." Vorster desired a "reasonable deal" for white Rhodesians that he could sell to both the Rhodesian prime leader, Ian Smith, and his own South African voters. This would have to include financial incentives to prevent a mass departure of whites, some guarantees of "minority rights," a "moderate" black leader, and an end to the guerrilla struggle. The devil would be in the specifics of such a program, but Kissinger now believed that his diplomacy could help the US gain a huge victory in Africa less than a year after one of its most humiliating failures.

Kissinger has been chastised for his contacts with the apartheid administration. In Kissinger's defence, it is apparent that, as with his Middle East talks, he began these conversations with an idea of what an accord in America's national interest and, coincidentally, in the political interest of the Ford administration would look like. He believed that Zambia's Kaunda or Tanzania's Nyerere would take Sadat's place as a moderate leader eager to interact with the reviled white dictatorship in the same way that Sadat had with the despised Jewish state. He would treat South Africa similarly to how he had treated Israel, offering sympathy and reassurance while insisting on tough compromises, initially at the expense of white Rhodesians but later on issues such as Namibia, which South Africa still controlled, and the apartheid system itself. Kissinger was referring to step-by-step diplomacy in both the Middle East and South Africa, usually by leaving some "creative ambiguity" in the terms of the accords he addressed while pushing the process along. Unfortunately, Kissinger's techniques, like any incremental approach to a moral issue, are always susceptible to criticism from people who desire more immediate and broad action but may misjudge the hurdles and human costs that action may entail.

Kissinger departed Vorster's meeting and returned to America, but not before briefing Prime Minister James Callaghan and Foreign Secretary Anthony Crosland in Britain. The United States and Britain worked out the details of the arrangement to give to the Smith government over the next two months. Some British officials were concerned that Kissinger, in his rush to reach an agreement before the American elections, was misrepresenting the willingness of the white Rhodesians and African states to cooperate. With the Ford-Reagan election still undecided, Kissinger avoided resolving issues in order to avoid anything that the Reagan opposition may denounce. He even went on a tour through rural Southwest Asia in the weeks before the Republican National Convention in mid-August, visiting Pakistan and Afghanistan while staying out of the news. He returned to attend the convention's last day. The ratification of the "Morality in Foreign Policy" platform plank by the convention was a devastating blow to Kissinger, with its condemnation of his détente tactics and laud of Aleksandr Solzhenitsyn as a "great beacon of human courage." "How can the President permit this to happen and not look like a weak coward?" Kissinger questioned Rockefeller. His rage is also visible in his vehement reaction to the North Korean "tree-cutting attack," in which North Korean forces viciously attacked American soldiers who had entered the demilitarised zone to prune a tree, killing two Americans. Kissinger desired a much stronger response, including the shelling of North Korean camps. Ford rejected such options in favour of just returning to the DMZ and chopping down the tree. Kissinger told Scowcroft, "Do you think I made it clear to the president how unenchanted I was with him?" after making a crude joke about utilising the tree's wood as coffins for the slain soldiers. As upset and frustrated as Kissinger was with Ford's reaction to the Korean crisis and his failure to defend Kissinger's foreign policy, he still urgently wanted the president to win. Kissinger told Ford on August 30, after the convention had ended and the campaign had begun, "What we need to think about is your political situation." Americans, in my opinion, do not like blacks. "I don't want to be in another Texas situation." Americans would see things differently if Kissinger could get South African cooperation, Ford said. He went on to say, "I think if it is right, we should do it and the political consequences will come out alright." The president concluded the discussion by telling his secretary of state, "Now that we've gotten rid of that son-of-a-bitch Reagan, we can do what's right."

Kissinger left for Zurich to speak with Vorster again and persuade him to deliver Ian Smith. Vorster accepted the responsibility, and Kissinger promised to travel to South Africa to meet with Smith personally. During a news conference following the meeting, Kissinger tried to avoid using words that could be interpreted as an unpleasant comparison to "peace is near." "Should I say, 'progress' is at hand?" he joked with reporters. Although Kissinger desired African success for Ford's campaign, he also knew that it would boost his credibility if he could claim bipartisan support for his approach. When he returned to Washington, he approached former Secretary of State Dean Rusk with the hopes of using him as a conduit to the Carter campaign. Because the American financial commitment to assist pay the transition to majority rule was a critical aspect in the negotiations, he wanted to see if Jimmy Carter would agree to refrain from criticising the administration's African strategy. Carter requested guarantees that African leaders and Congress would be kept aware of Kissinger's conversations, and then agreed not to address the matter further. Kissinger told Rusk, "I think he's behaving very patriotically." Carter's patriotism is obvious, but the decision may have been made simpler because, at the time of Kissinger's request, the Democrat was polling nearly thirty points ahead of Ford.

The following week, Kissinger returned to Africa, and his return to shuttle diplomacy was the headline story on all three television networks. The significance of Kissinger's efforts was also evident in the coverage of the country's continuous bloodshed, which had extended throughout the country. A strike shut down Cape Town's harbour two days before Kissinger was scheduled to arrive in Pretoria. Kissinger travelled to the capitals of two African frontline states, Tanzania and Zambia, where he was met with violent demonstrations and scepticism from their leaders about his possibilities of brokering a settlement. The evening news continued to emphasise the grave dangers of race conflict in southern Africa. President Kaunda informed American journalists that Kissinger had only "days left to avert a race war." Kissinger then became the first American secretary of state to visit South Africa, despite the bleak outlook. In a report to Ford, he stated that "after [his] seven painful hours of meetings with Ian Smith," the Rhodesians had "substantially accepted our proposals." The agreement to attain majority rule within two years was the primary concession. Negotiations would begin immediately on an interim government that "shares power, giving blacks a majority of the Cabinet but providing whites with the safeguard of a 50-50 split on a key executive body, the Council of State." In exchange, UN sanctions and the guerrilla war would be lifted, which the Rhodesians and South Africans considered as a "package" deal.

Printed in Great Britain
by Amazon